D0876517

YESHIVATH BETH MOSHE OF SCRANTON
is proud of its many contributions to
Torah scholarship. Since its beginning
in 1965, the Scranton Yeshiva has elevated the
calibre of Torah education through its high school,
beis medrash and Kollel-Graduate Program.

Our alumni rank among the leading
educators and lay leaders in America.

Over the years, dissemination of valuable,
informative and spiritually uplifting Jewish literature
has become a tradition at Beth Moshe.
It is in this tradition that we present with pride
this current volume.

RAMBAM
Selected Letters of Maimonides

Letter to Yemen
Discourse on Martyrdom

Translated and Annotated by
AVRAHAM YAAKOV FINKEL

YESHIVATH BETH MOSHE
SCRANTON, PA.

ISBN 0-9626226-3-X

Table of Contents

Foreword

Rabbeinu Moshe ben Maimon, better known as the Rambam (Maimonides), is considered one of the greatest codifiers and philosophers in Jewish history. He was born in Cordova, Spain in 1135. When Cordova was conquered by the fanatical Almohad Moslems, in 1148, the Rambam's family was forced to flee. They settled in Cairo in 1165. There the Rambam rose to prominence and became the undisputed leader of his generation and a towering guide of the generations to come. The Rambam died in Cairo in 1204.

The Rambam is the author of the seminal Mishneh Torah, a fourteen-volume compilation of all Torah laws, called Yad Hachazakah. He also wrote Commentary on the Mishnah, Moreh Nevuchim—a classical philosophical work—and many other writings. These writings have been accessible for nearly 800 years—but only to those familiar with the Hebrew language. We at Yeshiva Beth Moshe have endeavored to present some of these writings in a language compatible to those of us who speak and read English.

We are indebted to the well known writer, Rabbi Avraham Yaakov Finkel, for his diligence and expertise in this venture. He is always a pleasure to work with, and his concern for the Yeshiva is most appreciated.

We also wish to acknowledge our sincere appreciation to Dr. Jeff & Mrs. Bonnie Berman for taking time out of their busy schedule to edit this book.

A special thank you to Mrs. Sora Epstein who made herself available at all hours typing and retyping this book. We also want to acknowledge the help given by Mrs. Tzippy Prero, Mrs. Chava Pick, Mrs. Rivkie Hamada and Mrs. Esther Flam on this project.

Our special thanks to Mr. Solomon Swimer of Zeved Graphics, and Cy Munn for the beautiful graphics and layout of this series.

YESHIVA BETH MOSHE, Adar, 5754

Iggeres Teiman
The Letter to the Jews of Yemen

Preface

Iggeres Teiman, The Letter to the Jews of Yemen, written in 1172 in Arabic, is the Rambam's response to an inquiry from Rabbi Yaakov ben Nesanel Fayumi, the leader of the Jewish community of Yemen. The Jews of that far-off country were beset at that time by harrowing misfortunes. A fanatical Shi'ite Moslem rebel had risen to power and was forcing the Jews to convert to Islam. The alternative was death or expulsion. At the same time, a Jewish apostate, who became a missionary for Islam, was trying to win converts among the Yemenite Jews by spouting spurious scriptural proofs to confirm the genuineness of Mohammed's message. To make matters worse, a man purporting to be Mashiach appeared on the scene. He was misleading the unlearned masses and gained a large following among them. In utter confusion, many Yemenite Jews tried to calculate the date of the coming of Mashiach by means of astrology.

The Rambam, who had himself experienced the ordeals of persecution and forced conversion, sent his reply, in the form of The Letter to the Jews of Yemen. With great wisdom and deep sensitivity he addressed each of the problems facing that community. He explained the grandeur of the Torah and magnificence of the Jewish people. He revealed the fallacy of other doctrines and astrology, and the idiocy of the apostate's so-called proofs. He concluded his letter with a discussion of the characteristics of the true Mashiach, and the criteria by which Mashiach can be recognized.

At the Rambam's request, Iggeres Teiman was read in public gatherings in every city and village. Its inspiring words had a tremendous effect on the Jews of Yemen. Infused with hope and pride in their heritage, they resolved to remain faithful to Judaism and ignore the arguments of missionaries and the "miracles" of fraudulent Messiahs.

So grateful was the Yemenite community to the Rambam for his Iggeres that they bestowed on him the highest honor; inserting his name in the Kaddish prayer, including in it the phrase, *"bechayeichon uveyomeichon* **uvechayei deRabbi Moshe ben Maimon** . . . during your lifetime and during your days and during the lifetime of Rabbi Moshe ben Maimon . . ."

It is interesting to note that through the centuries, from the time of the Rambam until the present, the Jews of Yemen, despite ceaseless persecution, harassment and oppression, proudly have clung to the traditions of their fathers and are known for their scrupulous observance of the Torah and all mitzvos.

Iggeres Teiman
Letter to Yemen

Rambam's Introduction

By Moshe son of Rabbi Maimon, the Judge,
son of Rabbi Yosef,
son of Rabbi Yitzchak,
son of Rabbi Ovadiah, the Judge.
To strengthen the hands that are slack;
and make firm tottering knees!

To the holy, wise, congenial and distinguished scholar, Rabbi Yaakov al-Fayumi, son of the distinguished Rabbi Nesanel al-Fayumi, to all the communal leaders and scholars of the communities of Yemen: may Hashem, the Rock, keep and protect them. Amen. Selah.

1

Praising the Yemenite Community

Stems attest to the integrity of their roots, and streams bear witness to the excellence of their springs. So too, has a faithful twig sprouted out of a root of truth. A mighty river has flowed out of the wellspring of kindness in the land of Yemen to water all gardens and make blossoms flourish[1]. It flows leisurely to quench the thirst of every weary and thirsty wanderer in the wilderness. It satisfies the needs of all travelers on the roads and distant islands. So the message was heralded throughout Spain and beyond from one end of heaven to the other, *"All who are thirsty, come for water.*[2]*"* Unanimously, all wayfarers reported that they had found in the land of Yemen a beautiful, luscious garden. They found a rich pasture where every shriveled creature becomes fat, a dependable grazing-ground for their shepherds. The [Jews of Yemen] share their bread with the poor; they welcome the rich and offer them hospitality. Caravans from Sheba count on them[3]; they stretch out their hands to every voyager. Their homes are wide open. Everyone finds there tranquility and solace from sorrow and sighs[4]. They study the Torah all day and follow in the path of Rav Ashi[5]. They pursue justice and maintain their synagogues in good repair. They restore the principles of the Torah to their former glory. With kind words they

---

1   These sentences are meant to praise both Rabbi Yaakov Al-Fayumi and his father.
2.   Ref. to *Yeshayah 55:1*
3.   Ref. to *Iyov 6:19*
4.   Ref. to *Yeshayah 35:10*
5.   Rav Ashi was a leading Amora, (Talmudic authority), who together with Ravina, compiled and edited the Talmud. For almost sixty years he led the yeshivah of Masa Mechasya, near Sura in Babylonia.

bring back to Hashem those who have strayed, and fulfill all mitzvos meticulously. There is no breach and no defection, and no wailing in their streets[6].

Blessed is Hashem for not depriving the distant isles (Yemen) of Jews who observe the Torah and keep its law, as He promised in His goodness and mercy through His servant Yeshayah. You [the Yemenite Jewish community] are the people that [Yeshayah] had in mind when he announced, *"From the end of the earth we hear singing" (Yeshayah 24:16)*. May Hashem help you to fulfill the laws and precepts of the Torah, to heed justice and righteousness, to guard His mitzvos and decrees, and to uphold His covenant. Amen.

When your esteemed letter reached us in Egypt[7], everyone was delighted to hear of it and enjoyed reading it. It told us that you are servants of Hashem who are standing in His Sanctuary and camping under His banner. You pursue the study of the Torah, love its laws, and wait at its doors[8]. May Hashem reveal its hidden treasures to you and fill your hearts with its riches. May its words be a lamp to your feet and a light for your path.

Denies Lavish Praises

Beloved friends, You state that you heard fellow Jews in the lands of our exile—may God protect

---

6. Ref. to Tehillim 144:14
7. In 1172, when the Rambam wrote the Iggeres Teiman, he was the chief rabbi of Cairo and spiritual leader of all Egyptian Jewry.
8. Ref. to Mishlei 8:34

them—praise me, extol me and rate me as a towering scholar. They only said this out of love for me and spoke this way out of the goodness of their hearts and their kindness. Let me give you the facts. Do not listen to anyone else.

I am one of the humblest of scholars of Spain whose prestige was lowered in exile. Although I always study the teachings of the Torah, I did not reach the level of learning of my ancestors because evil days and hard times came upon us. We have not lived in tranquility. We were exhausted but were given no rest. I have pursued the reapers in their paths and gathered ears of grain, both the solid and the full ones, as well as the shriveled and the thin ones. Only recently have I found a home[9]. Were it not for the help of Hashem, I would not have attained the small amount of knowledge that I gathered and from which I continually draw.

Concerning my dear friend and student Rabbi Shlomoh Cohen who, according to your letter, praised me exceedingly, he exaggerates out of his great love for me.

May Zion and Jerusalem be rebuilt and become a flourishing garden. May Hashem return it to us in good health and happiness.

[The rhymed preface was written in Hebrew. The remainder of the Letter to Yemen was written in Arabic and translated into Hebrew by Rabbi Shmuel ibn Tibbon, in 1210. A second translation was written by Rabbi Nachum Ma'arabi (of the Maghreb)[10] and appeared in Basel, Switzerland, in 1629.]

9.   Fleeing from persecution, the Rambam left his native Spain, traveled to Fez, Morocco, to Eretz Yisrael, and at last settled in Egypt.
10. The Maghreb is a region in NW Africa, consisting mainly of Morocco, Algeria and Tunisia (compare with the Hebrew ma'ariv, "west"); it usually means just Morocco.

Regarding the subject matter of your letter about which you asked for a response, I thought it best to reply in Arabic so that all—men, women and children alike—should be able to read and understand it. The answer is of primary concern to your entire community.

Words of Consolation

Bemoaning the Fate of the Yemenite Jews

You write that the rebel leader in Yemen[1] forced the Jews to convert to Islam. He compelled the inhabitants of all the places under his control to abandon their religion. This is just as the Berber leader has done in the lands of the Maghreb[2]. This news has appalled us and has caused our entire community to tremble and shudder. And with good right, for these are indeed bad tidings, and both ears of anyone who hears about it will tingle[3]. Yes, our hearts are faint and

---

1. His name is Abd el-Nabi ibn Mahdi. In c. 1170 he conquered Yemen and forced all Jews to convert to Islam.
2. The Berber Almohads, (from 1150-1180), forced the Jews of Morocco to convert to Islam.
3. Ref. to Shmuel I 3:11

our minds are confused because of these dreadful calamities which brought forced conversion on our people in the two ends of the world, the East and the West[4]. The Jewish people are caught in the middle and are under attack from both sides[5].

It was a vision of this dreadful time that inspired the prophet to plead and pray for us, stating, *"I said, 'O Lord God, stop! How will Yaakov survive? He is so small'"* *(Amos 7:5)*. This persecution should not cause one whose faith in Hashem is strong to come to doubt or one who believes in Moshe to waver. There can be no doubt that these are the pangs of the Age of Mashiach about which the Sages begged Hashem that they be spared from suffering. The prophets trembled when they foresaw them. As it is stated, *"My mind is confused, I shudder in panic. The twilight that I longed for has turned to terror" (Yeshayah 21:4)*. Hashem Himself in the Torah exclaims His sympathy for those who will experience the times preceding Mashiach, stating, *"Alas, who can survive God's devastation!" (Bamidbar 24:23)*.

You write that the minds of some people have become clouded. As uncertainty grips their hearts, their faith begins to waver, and their hope falters. Others have not lost faith and have neither weakened nor become fearful.

Regarding this matter, we have a Divine prophecy by Daniel. He foretold that as a result of the long stay in exile and the continuous persecutions, many would forsake our faith as doubt entered their minds and made them go astray. The primary reason for this breakdown is that they witnessed our weakness in contrast to the power of our oppressors and their mas-

---

4. Yemen and Morocco
5. Ref. to Yehoshua 8:22

tery over us. Others would not be plagued by doubts. Their belief would remain firm and unshaken. This is expressed in the verse, *"Many will be purified and purged and refined; the wicked will act wickedly and none of the wicked will understand; but the knowledgeable will understand" (Daniel 12:10)*. Daniel also prophesied that even these knowledgeable people and men of understanding who would have put up with milder misfortunes and remained steadfast in their faith in God and His servant Moshe, would give way to disbelief and would stray when they were made to endure harsher and more severe afflictions. Only a few of them would remain pure in faith, as it is stated, *"Some of the knowledgeable will stumble, that they may be refined and purged and whitened until the time of the end, for an interval still remains until the appointed time" (Daniel 11:35)*.

Two Strategies

And now, dear brothers, it is essential that you pay attention and listen to what I am about to present to you. Teach it to your wives and children, so their faith which has been weakened by misgivings, may be strengthened. May their souls be bolstered by the unshakable truth. May Hashem save us and all of you from religious doubt!

Bear in mind that our Torah is the true Divine Teaching that was given to us through Moshe, the master of both the early and the later prophets. By means of His Torah, God has distinguished us from the rest of mankind. As it says, *"It was only with your ancestors that Hashem developed a closeness. He loved them and therefore chose you, their descendants, from among all nations—as is now the case" (Devarim 10:15).* This did not happen because we were worthy of it. Rather, it was an act of Divine kindness, because our forefathers recognized Hashem and worshipped Him. As it says, *"It was not because you had greater numbers than all the other nations that Hashem preferred you . . . It was because of Hashem's love for you, and because He was keeping the oath He made to your fathers" (Devarim 7:7).*

Hashem made us special through His laws and decrees. The other nations recognize our superiority because we are guided by His rules and statutes. As it says, *"[The nations will say,] 'What nation is so great that they have such righteous rules and laws'" (Devarim 4:8).* As a result, the nations of the world became terribly envious of us. Because of the Torah, all the kings of the earth stirred up hatred and jealousy against us. Their real intention is to make war against Hashem, but no one can oppose the Almighty. Ever since the time of the Giving of the Torah, every non-Jewish king, no matter how he rose to power, has made it his first objective to destroy the Torah. Amalek, Sisera, Sancheriv, Nebuchadnezzar, Titus, Hadrian, and many others like them, tried to overturn our religion by force, by violence and by the sword. [The nations who want to annihilate us through violence] are one of two groups whose aim is to defeat the Divine will.

The second group consists of the brightest and most educated among the nations, such as the Syrians, Persians and Greeks. They also attempt to tear down our religion and wipe out our Torah [but they do it] by means of arguments they offer and questions they dream up. They try to demolish the Torah and to erase its last trace with their writings. The tyrants tried to do the same with their wars.

Neither the one nor the other will succeed. Hashem

proclaimed through the prophet Yeshayah, that He will destroy the armaments of any despot or oppressor who intends to destroy our Torah and abolish our religion by weapons of war. In the same way, whenever a disputant will argue to undermine our religion, he will lose the debate. His theory will be exploded and refuted. This thought is expressed in the following verse, *"No weapon formed against you will succeed, and every tongue that contends with you at law you will defeat. Such is the lot of the servants of Hashem, such is their triumph through Me—declares Hashem" (Yeshayah 54:17).*

Although advocates of both strategies (compulsory conversion and conversion through argumentation) realized that [Judaism] is a structure that cannot easily be demolished, they made a concerted effort to tear down its solid foundations. They are only increasing their toil and pain while the structure remains as strong as ever. Hashem, who is the Truth, mocks and ridicules them, because, with their feeble intelligence they try to reach an unattainable goal. Observing their attempt to wreck the true faith and watching Hashem ridicule them, David was inspired to say, *"[About those that say:] 'Let us break the cords of their yoke, shake off their ropes from us!' He who is enthroned in heaven laughs; Hashem mocks at them" (Tehillim 2:3).* Both groups have troubled and tormented us without letup throughout the era of our independence and during part of the period of our exile.

After that, a new sect arose which made our lives miserable by combining the approaches of the two groups: brute force and persuasion. It believed that this method would be more effective in wiping out the last vestige of the Jewish nation. It, therefore, conceived a plan to claim divine revelation and establish a new religion, contrary to our God-given Torah. It declared publicly that both revelations were given by

God. It meant to raise doubts and sow confusion. The new religion claimed to believe in the same God but to be the recipients of a new set of commandments. Thereby it hoped to destroy our Torah.

The first one who devised this plan was Jeshu the Nazarene, may his bones be crushed. He was a Jew because his mother was Jewish although his father was a gentile. Our law states that a child born of a Jewish woman and a gentile or a slave is a kosher Jew. We only call him a *mamzer* (illegitimate child) in a manner of speaking. He led people to believe that he was sent by Hashem to explain bewildering passages in the Torah, and that he was the Mashiach who was predicted by each and every prophet. He interpreted the Torah in a way that would invalidate it completely, do away with all its mitzvos, and sanction all its prohibitions. The Sages guessed his purpose before his fame spread among the people, and condemned him to receive the punishment he deserved. Daniel predicted his emergence when he spoke of the downfall of a renegade and heretic who would arise in Yisrael. He spoke of one who would attempt to destroy the Torah and boast of having prophetic powers, of being able to perform miracles and who would declare himself as Mashiach, as it says, *"The lawless sons of your people will assert themselves to claim prophecy, but they will fail (Daniel 11:14).*

Long after he lived, the descendants of Eisav created a religion and traced its origins to him. He did not establish a new faith, and did not actually do any harm to Yisrael, since neither the community as a whole nor any individuals were shaken in their beliefs because of him. His flaws were obvious to everyone. He fell into our hands and his fate is known to all.

After him, the Madman (Mohammed) arose. He followed in his forerunner's footsteps and attempted to convert us. He had the added ambition of pursuing political power, seeking to subjugate the people under his rule, and he originated his well-known religion [of Islam].

The Superiority of the Torah

These men had one purpose: to place their false religions on the same level with our Divine faith. Only a child who knows nothing about either religion would equate our God-given faith to man-made theories. Our religion is as different from other religions as a living, thinking human being differs from a wooden, metal or stone statue that looks like a man. On the surface and in its shape, form and appearance the statue looks exactly like man. The simple-minded person who knows nothing of Divine wisdom or of the art of sculpture, thinks that it is made the same way man is made; he does not understand the inner workings of both. A knowledgeable person, who knows the inner nature of both, knows that the internal structure of the statue does not manifest any skillful workmanship at all. The inner parts of man are the true wonders that reveal the wisdom of the Creator: the nerves extending into the muscles which allow man to move his limbs at will; the attachment of ligaments, how they cling to bone, and the manner in which they grow; the connection of bones and joints; blood vessels that pulsate and those that do not and how they branch out; the placement of man's organs overlapping one another; how every part of the body has its proper composition, form and place.

Similarly, a person unfamiliar with the Holy Scriptures' secret meaning and the commandments deeper significance may think that our religion has something in common with, or is comparable to, the spurious man-made faith. He is misled. Both in Judaism and in the false religion there are things that you may not do and things that you must do; both in Judaism and the false religion there are various forms of worship. The Torah provides many positive and negative commandments, punishment and reward, and so does the fraudulent, man-made religion.

But if he knew the deeper meaning of the commandments, he would realize that the God-given Torah is true. It is the essence of Divine wisdom. Every commandment and prohibition moves man closer to perfection and removes the barriers that prevent him from attaining excellence. Through these commandments, both the broad masses and the individual will be able to reach moral and intellectual refinement, each according to his ability and perception. Through the mitzvos, the community of God becomes elevated, reaching a twofold perfection. By the first perfection, I mean living in this world under the most pleasant and gratifying conditions. The second perfection is the attainment of intellectual heights for each person according to his ability.

The other religions that resemble our religion really have no deeper meaning. They are only stories and imaginary tales in which the founder is trying to glorify himself, stating that he is as great as so-and-so. The Sages saw through the deception. They saw the entire religion as a farce and a joke, just as people laugh at a monkey who apes the actions of men.

Proofs From the Prophets

Hashem made it known to us through Daniel that something like this would happen in the future. He revealed to us that in the future, a person would arise who would announce a religion similar to the true one. He would speak haughtily. He would claim through prophetic powers that the prophetic spirit had given him a scripture, that God had spoken to him, that he had replied to Him, and many other claims such as these. Daniel had a vision of a horn that grew and became long and strong. In it, he prophesied the rise of the Arabic kingdom, the emergence of the Madman (Mohammed), and how he would triumph over the kingdoms of Syria, Persia and Greece. This is clearly shown in verses that can be understood by everyone. This interpretation is borne out by historical facts. The verses cannot be explained any other way. Daniel says, *"While I was gazing upon these horns, a new little horn sprouted up among them; three of the older horns were uprooted to make room for it... There were eyes in this horn like those of a man, and a mouth that spoke arrogantly"* (Daniel 7:8).

Now consider how marvelously fitting this allegory is. Daniel says that he saw a little horn sprouting. As he was wondering about its length and that it uprooted three horns, he noticed that this horn had eyes like those of a man and a mouth that spoke arrogantly. Clearly this refers to the person who will establish a religion that will resemble Hashem's Torah and who will claim to be a prophet. Daniel lets us know that this person wants to destroy, abolish and alter our Torah. He states, *"He will think of changing times and laws. They will be delivered into his power for a time, times, and half a time"* (Daniel 7:25).

Hashem informed Daniel that He would destroy this religion in spite of its greatness and the great length of its reign, together with the remnants of the nations that preceded it.

The three groups that tried to wipe us out: that is to say, the one that tried to overwhelm us with the sword, the second that sought to defeat us by arguments, and the third that founded a religion similar to ours, will perish in the end.

Although they will seem to be powerful and victorious for a while, their power will not last and their triumph will not endure. Hashem so ordained it. He promised us from time immemorial that whenever Jews are forced to convert or any evil decree is issued against us, He will in the end remove and abolish it. David saw, through Divine Spirit the future of the Jewish people. He saw heathen nations oppress us, rule over us, persecute us and try to force us into apostasy, but they were not able to annihilate us. He exclaimed in the name of Yisrael, *"Since my youth they have often assailed me, let Yisrael now declare; since my youth they have often assailed me, but they have never overcome me" (Tehillim 129:1,2).*

Parallels in History

My brothers, you all know that in the time of the wicked Nebuchadnezzar, the Jews were forced to worship idols. Only Daniel, Chananaiah, Mishael and Azariah were spared[6]. Yet ultimately, Hashem crushed

---

6. In the third chapter of Daniel, we are told that these three men refused to bow down to an idol. They were thrown into a fiery furnace and miraculously, they came out unscathed.

Nebuchadnezzar and abolished his laws, and the religion of truth was restored.

During the second Temple, when the wicked Greek kingdom came to power, the Greeks instituted brutal and harsh measures against Yisrael in order to destroy the Torah. They forced the Jews to desecrate the Shabbos and prohibited the observance of *bris milah* (circumcision). Every Jew was compelled to write on his garment the words, "We have no portion in Hashem, the God of Yisrael." He also had to etch this phrase on the horn of his ox and then to plow with it. These decrees were in force for about fifty-two years. After this time, Hashem demolished both their regime and their laws.

The Sages often refer to persecutions. We find, "Once the wicked Greek rulers forced the Jews to abandon their faith," and, "they issued such and such decree." After a while, Hashem would nullify and cancel the decree and obliterate the nation that issued it. Noting this historic pattern prompted the Sages of blessed memory to say, "Persecutions do not last" (Kesuvos 3b).

Hashem promised Yaakov that his offspring would outlive the nations who enslaved and oppressed them. They would survive and rise again while the tyrants would fade away, as it is written, *"Your descendants will be like the dust of the earth" (Bereishis 28:14)*. Although Yaakov's descendants will be degraded and stepped on like dust, eventually, they will win and emerge triumphant. In a metaphoric sense we can say, just as the dust finally settles on he who steps on it and exists long after he has perished, [so will Yisrael outlive their tormentors.]

Yeshayah foretold in Divine prophecy that while the Jewish people are in exile, any nation that wishes to overpower and oppress them will be successful. In the end Hashem will help the Jewish people. He will remove their affliction and pain. Yeshaya says, *"A harsh prophecy has been announced to me: 'The betrayer is betraying, the ravager ravaging. Advance, Elam! Lay siege Media! I will put an end to all her sighing"' (Yeshayah 21:2).*

Encouraging Words

Hashem has assured us through his prophets that Yisrael will never be destroyed and we will never stop being His treasured nation. Just as it is unthinkable for Hashem to cease to exist so is it impossible for Yisrael to be destroyed and annihilated. As it says, *"For I am Hashem—I have not changed; and you the children of Jacob—have not ceased to be"* (Malachi 3:6). He announced and confirmed to us that it is inconceivable that He will reject us entirely, even if we anger Him by violating His commandments. As it is written, *"Thus says Hashem, 'If the heavens above could be measured, and the foundations of the earth could be fathomed, only then would I reject all the offspring of Yisrael for all that they have done—declares Hashem'"* (Yirmiyah 31:37).

Indeed, the very same promise has been made to us in the Torah through Moshe our teacher: *"Thus even when they are in their enemies' land, I will not grow so disgusted with them nor so tired of them that I would destroy them and break My covenant with them, for I am Hashem their God"* (Vayikra 26:44).

Dear brothers, be strong and brave. Place your trust in these true Scriptures. Don't be disheartened by the persecutions that continually befall you. Don't be frightened by the power of our enemy and the help-lessness of our people. These trials are meant to test you and to prove your faith and your love of Hashem. The God-fearing Torah scholars of the pure and untainted lineage of Yaakov will remain faithful to the true religion in times like these. About these the prophet states, *"And among the remnant are those whom Hashem will call" (Yoel 3:5).* The prophet makes it clear that they are only a few individuals. They are the men whose ancestors stood at Mount Sinai and heard Hashem's words, entered into the covenant of Hashem, and took upon themselves to do and obey. They said, *"We will do and obey all that Hashem has declared" (Shemos 24:7).* They obligated not only them-selves but also their descendants, as we read, *"That which has been revealed applies to us and our children forev-er" (Devarim 29:28).* Hashem assured us, like a man who vouches for his neighbor—and we certainly can rely on His guarantee—that not only all those who stood at Mount Sinai [when Hashem gave the Torah] believe in the prophecy of Moshe our Teacher and in the laws he transmitted to us. Their descendants like-wise would do so, until the end of time. Hashem said, *"I will come to you in a thick cloud, so that all the people will hear when I speak to you. They will then believe in you for-ever' (Shemos 19:9).*

It follows, therefore, that anyone who rejects the re-ligion that was given at this Revelation at Sinai is not a descendant of the people who witnessed it. In the same vein, our Sages of blessed memory stated that whoever harbors doubts about the Divine prophecy is not a descendant of the people who were present at Mount Sinai (Nedarim 20a). May Hashem save me and you from doubt. May He keep away from all of us the thoughts that lead to skepticism and failure.

Advice for the Yemenite Jews

And so, dear brothers who are scattered through the far reaches of [Yemen], you should encourage one another. Let the elders hearten the youth and the leaders inspire the masses. Convince your community of the immutable and unalterable truth. Proclaim loudly that our faith will never fail and will never be destroyed. Announce publicly [the principles of our religion]:

"The Holy One Blessed is He is One. There is no other unity like His[1].

Moshe is His prophet who spoke with Him, he is the master of all prophets, and he is superior to all other prophets. He perceived the Godly surpassing every other prophet whether he preceded him or arose afterwards[2].

The entire Torah, starting from the verse *"In the beginning" (Bereishis 1:1)*, until the verse *"before the eyes of all Yisrael" (Devarim 34:12)*, was transmitted by Hashem to Moshe, as it says, *"With him I speak mouth to mouth" (Bamidbar 12:8)*[3].

[The Torah] will neither be revoked nor altered, nothing can ever be added or subtracted from it. Never will Hashem give another Torah or a new positive or negative commandment[4]."

Keep in mind that Hashem commanded us to remember and never to forget, the Revelation on Mount Sinai. He instructed us to teach this event to our chil-

---

1. The second of the Rambam's Thirteen Principles of the Jewish faith
2. The seventh principle of the Rambam's Thirteen Principles of the Jewish faith.
3. The eighth principle of the Rambam's Thirteen Principles of the Jewish faith.
4. The ninth principle of the Rambam's Thirteen Principles of the Jewish faith.

dren so that they will grow up with this lesson etched in their minds. As it is written, *"Only take heed and watch yourself very carefully, so that you do not forget the things that your eyes saw. Do not let [this memory] leave your hearts, all the days of your lives. Teach your children and children's children about the day that you stood before Hashem at Chorev"* (Devarim 4:9-10).

It is essential, my dear brothers, that you impress on your children's minds this momentous Stand at Sinai. Proclaim at mass meetings its overriding significance. Stress that it is the cornerstone of our faith and the proof of its truthfulness. Accentuate the pivotal importance of this event, as Hashem did in the verse, *"You might inquire about times long past, going back to the time that Hashem created man on earth, and from one end of the heavens to the other. See if anything as great as this has ever happened, or if the like has ever been heard"* (Devarim 4:32).

The Purpose of the Revelation at Sinai

Remember, my fellow Jews, the fact that [the Torah is of divine origin] is attested to by the best possible evidence. Never before or since has an entire nation heard the Divine Word or witnessed His glory with their own eyes. The purpose of this was to implant the faith firmly in us so that nothing can shake it, and to give us conviction that will uphold us so that we will not slip[5] in these trying times of recurring persecution

---

5.   Tehillim 37:31

and forced conversion, when our enemy will have gained the upper hand. As it is stated, *"For Hashem has come in order to test you, and in order that the fear of Him may be on your faces, so that you will not sin"* (Shemos 20:17). The verse explains that the reason Hashem revealed Himself to the Jewish people was in order to enable them to withstand all trials until the end of time. They will not be swayed and not be led astray. You, dear brothers, keep the faith, stay on course, and remain true to your belief.

Forced Apostasy Predicted in the Torah

King Shlomoh compared the Jewish people to a woman of matchless grace and flawless beauty. He stated, *"Every part of you is beautiful, my beloved, there is no blemish in you"* (Shir Hashirim 4:7). By contrast, he describes the followers of other religions and philosophies who want to lure us and convert us to their creed as worthless men. They seduce virtuous women in order to satisfy their depraved lust. This is exactly what they are doing to us when they beguile and ensnare us in their web of deceit and falsehood. These nations try to lead the Jewish people astray by contending that their religion is better than the Jewish faith. Yisrael says to them in rebuttal, *"Why do you take hold of me? Have you anything to show like 'the encirclement of the two camps?'"* (Shir Hashirim 7:1). The meaning of this metaphor is, "Show me something, as magnificent as the Revelation on Sinai in which the camp of Yisrael faced the camp of the Divine Presence.

Then we will accept your teaching."

This thought is allegorically expressed in the verses, *"[The Gentile nations say to Yisrael[6]:] 'Turn away, turn away [from Hashem], Shulamis! Turn away, turn away, that we may gaze upon you, [we shall choose nobility for you].' [But Yisrael replies:] 'What can you bestow on Shulamis that can equal mecholas hamachanaim [literally, the encirclement of the two camps]?'"* (Shir Hashirim 7:1).

Now, the name *Shulamis* signifies "the nation whose faith in Hashem is perfect[7]". The expression *mecholas hamachanaim,*signifies "the encirclement of the two camps". This alludes to the joy of the Stand at Sinai which was shared by both the camp of Yisrael and the camp of Hashem. As we see in the following verses: *"Moshe led the people out of the camp toward the Divine Presence. They stood transfixed at the foot of the mountain."* (Shemos 19:17), and *"Hashem's chariots are myriads upon myriads, thousands upon thousands; Hashem is among them as in Sinai in holiness"* (Tehillim 68:18).

Now pay close attention to the fitting imagery and the deeper meaning of the verse [in Shir Hashirim]. Note that the phrase *turn away* is repeated four times. This alludes to the four empires that will try to force us to abandon our faith. Incidentally, we are living today under the domination of the fourth and last empire.

In the Torah, Hashem foretold that while [we are in exile, the nations of the world] would compel us to embrace their religion. As it says, *"There you will serve Gods that men have made"* (Devarim 4:28). However, this will not happen all over the world; we will never be completely cut off from the Torah. Hashem gave us His assurance. He stated, *"[The Torah] will not be forgot-*

6. Commentary between brackets is Rashi's interpretation of this verse.
7. From the root *shalem*, "perfect."

ten by their descendants" (Devarim 31:21). Yeshayah, the harbinger of our nation's redemption, already declared that the Divine guarantee of our survival as a nation is the permanence of the Torah among us. As it is written, *"'And as for Me, this is My covenant with them,' said Hashem. 'My spirit that is upon you and My words that I have placed in your mouth shall not be absent from your mouth, nor out of the mouth of your children nor from the mouth of your children's children' said Hashem, 'from now on, for all time'"* (Yeshayah 59:21).

Our Response

With pride, our nation speaks to Hashem of the dreadful oppression and persecution it has suffered. We state, *"It is for Your sake that we are killed all day long, that we are regarded as sheep to be led to slaughter"* (Tehillim 44:23). The Sages comment that the phrase, "It is for Your sake that we are killed all day long," refers to the generation that suffers forced apostasy (Midrash Shir Hashirim 1:3).

We should rejoice in the fact that we have suffered misfortune, lost our wealth and possessions and were driven into exile. All these hardships are a source of distinction and honor in the eyes of Hashem. Whatever losses we suffered through these disasters are counted as a burnt offering on the altar. The following verse[8] expresses this thought: *"Dedicate yourselves to Hashem today, . . . that He may bestow a blessing on you"* (Shemos 32:29).

---

8.   As translated by Targum Onkelos.

[Those who are being pressured into converting] should run away and remain faithful to Hashem. They should flee into the desert and hide in uninhabited places. They should give no thought of being separated from family and friends or being concerned with loss of income. Such deprivations are only a small sacrifice and a trifle [we can offer] to the King of kings, the Holy One, Blessed is He, Ruler of the universe, whose Name is glorious and awesome, Hashem your God. He can be trusted to give you a rich reward in this world and in the world to come.

Many pious and pure-hearted people, who seek the truth and pursue it, follow the practice of [leaving home and family]. They leave [society] behind. They advance from the far reaches of the world to the place where the word of Hashem is manifest. They make their way to the homes of the pious sages. They want to gain a deeper understanding of the Torah and earn a rich reward from Hashem. How much more so is one obligated to leave his homeland and his family, if it means preserving the Torah in its entirety.

Sometimes when a man cannot earn a livelihood in one country, he becomes disgusted with it, he feels cramped and fenced in, and he moves to another country. Surely, when a Jew is prevented from observing the Torah and the Divine faith, he should run away to another place. If he finds it impossible to leave at the present, he should not gradually backslide, lapse into sin and feel free to desecrate the Shabbos and eat forbidden foods. He should not think that he is exempt from observing the laws of the Torah. Whether he likes it or not, every descendant of Yaakov, as well as his children and children's offspring, is forever and inescapably bound to the Torah. Furthermore, a violator will be punished for every negative commandment he transgresses. Let no one think that since he was forced to commit some major sins he can freely and with impunity violate the commandments with the lesser penalties. *Yerovam ben Nevat*, may his bones be crushed, was punished, not only for erecting the two golden calves which he worshipped and enticed Yisrael to worship, he was also punished for his failure to observe the mitzvah of building a *sukkah* on *Sukkos*. This is one of the fundamental principles of the Torah and our religion. Master it, and apply it to your own situation.

Refuting Moslem Claims

The Fallacy of Moslem Arguments

In your letter you mention that the apostate intro-
duced doubt in the minds of several people. He
claimed that a number of verses in the Torah allude to
the Madman (Mohammed).

With the verse, *"I will bless him (Yishmael), and make
him fruitful, increasing his numbers* bimeod meod ——
very greatly"(Bereishis 17:20), Moslem apologists contend that *bimeod meod* which sounds like
Muchammad, is an allusion to Mohammed. They also
contend, that the numeric value of both *bimeod meod*
and Muchammad is 92.

They argue that the verse, *"He appeared from Mount
Paran" (Devarim 33:2)*, alludes to Mohammed. [Since
Mount Paran is a reference to Yishmael, son of
Avraham, and ancestor of the Arab nation, who lived
in the wilderness of Paran.]

They also believe that the passage, *"Hashem your God will raise up for you a prophet from among you, from your brothers, like myself" (Devarim 18:15),*and the promise to Yishmael, *"I will make him into a great nation" (Bereishis 17:20),* refer to Mohammed.

These arguments have been bandied about so much that everyone is sick and tired of them. To say that they are absolutely unsound is an understatement. To use these verses as proofs is ludicrous and outrageous. Such statements do not confuse anyone, not even the gullible masses.

The apostates who amuse themselves by concocting these "scriptural proofs" do not believe a word of them. They do not even entertain any doubts about their veracity. Their purpose in quoting these verses is to creep into the good graces of the Moslems and ingratiate themselves with them by showing that they are believers. Even knowledgeable Moslems do not believe these proofs. In trying to support the statement of the Koran that the Madman (Mohammed) is mentioned in the Torah, they don't rely on or accept these arguments. Clearly these proofs are worthless. The Moslems, when they could not find a single usable proof in the Torah—even by inference or hint—were forced to say that we revised and edited the Torah, deleting every mention of the name (Mohammed) from it. They could not find a more tenable argument in support of the Koran, even though it is absolutely absurd and does not hold water.

It is obvious to one and all [that nothing was deleted from the Torah], for the following reasons: First, the Torah was translated into Aramaic, Persian, Greek and Latin hundreds of years before the emergence of the *pasul,* the Defective One" (Mohammed). Second, the Torah text has been transmitted from generation to generation, both in the East and the West. There has never been found the slightest difference in the text, not even in the vocalization. There exists not even a variation between a *kametz chataf* and a *shuruk*[1]. The Moslems only used this feeble argument, because they could not find any inference to Mohammed in the Torah.

Yitzchak is Heir to Avraham's Blessing

As for the true meaning of the verse, *"I will make of him (Yishmael) a great nation" (Bereishis 17:20)*; the word "great" does not denote greatness in wisdom and prophecy. It only refers to vastness in numbers. Similarly, the Torah describes idol worshippers as, *"nations greater and more populous than you" (Devarim 4:38)*.

What of the promise to Yishmael, *"[I will increase his number]* bimeod meod—*very greatly," (Bereishis 17:20)?* If this Scripture intended to predict that Mohammed would descend from Yishmael it would have said, "I will bless him *bimeod meod*—very greatly." A very weak argument could then be made to interpret this to mean, "I will bless him by making Mohammed (which sounds like *bimeod meod*) one of his descendants." But since the phrase *bimeod meod* follows after *"I will increase his number,"* it is clear that this is intended only as a superlative, as if to say, "exceedingly numerous".

Hashem clearly explained to Avraham that all Divine promises regarding blessings and command-

1. Two similar sounding vowels.

ments to be given to his offspring and their separateness from the nations refer only to Yitzchak's descendants not to the other one (Yishmael). Yishmael's blessing comes only as an adjunct and is secondary to Yitzchak's blessing. This is evident in the passage, *"Also I will make the son of the slave-woman into a nation, for he is your child" (Bereishis 21:13).* This passage clearly places Yitzchak in first place, making the other one (Yishmael) inferior. In addition, the Torah expressly spells it out, *"It is through Yitzchak that there will be called for you a lineage" (Bereishis 21:12).* Even if we were to concede that Yishmael's offspring would be very great in numbers, they would still not be renowned and acclaimed for their qualities of righteousness and human perfection. On the other hand, Yitzchak's descendants will be celebrated for their righteousness. This is implied in the expression *yikarei lecha*—"will be called for you." This expression signifies fame and renown, as in *"veyikarei vahem shemi*—In them may my name be called" (Bereishis 48:16), meaning, "May my name become famous through them."

Regarding the blessings, Hashem specifically sets forth that these were given to Avraham. Included in this blessing was that the covenant and the Torah would exist in his descendants. Hashem put it into these words, *"To you and your descendants I will give the land where you are now living as a foreigner. The whole land of Canaan shall be your eternal heritage, and I will be a God to your descendants" (Bereishis 17:8).* Hashem singled out Yitzchak. Yishmael was excluded from all the blessings.

He then specifically selected Yitzchak for a covenant, eliminating Yishmael, as it says, *"But My covenant I will maintain* **with Yitzchak"** *(Bereishis 17:20).* Hashem then bestowed a blessing on Yishmael, stating, *"I will bless him and make him fruitful," (Bereishis*

17:20). The process of the transmission of the blessings is later clarified by Yitzchak when he passed on Avraham's blessings to Yaakov, leaving out Eisav. Yitzchak phrased his blessing to Yaakov in the following terms, *"May He grant the blessing of Avraham to you and your offspring" (Bereishis 28:4)*.

It is now abundantly clear that the pledges Hashem made to Avraham and his descendants would be fulfilled exclusively in first Yitzchak and then in Yaakov, Yitzchak's son. This is confirmed by a passage which states, *"He is ever mindful of His covenant . . . that He made with Avraham, swore to Yitzchak, and confirmed in a decree for Yaakov, for Yisrael, as an eternal covenant (Tehillim 105:8,9)*.

Point by Point Refutation of Moslem Allegations

Let me point out that the idea the Moslems have adopted that the name Mohammed occurs in the Torah—a notion that was dreamed up by the apostates—is senseless. They claim that the phrase *bimeod meod* alludes to Muchammad. But the name that is used in the Koran and the "Gospels[3]" is Achmed. And of course, the numeric value of *bimeod meod*—92—is not the same as that of Achmed, which is 53.

With regard to the so-called proof of *"hofia me'har Paran* -He appeared from Mount Paran" (Devarim 33:1), *hofia*—"he appeared" is written in the past

---

2.   The Rambam uses the word *avon galui*—"an open sin," as a play on the
      Greek word *evangelion* which means "good tidings" or gospels.

tense. If it would have read *"yofia*—He **will** appear,"
the Moslem spokesman might have used the passage
to taunt us and lend credence to his belief, but the
word *"hofia*—He **appeared**," points to an event that
happened in the past. In fact, it refers to the Giving of
the Torah on Mount Sinai. It is telling us that when
Hashem revealed Himself on Mount Sinai, He did not
plummet down from heaven like a barrage of hail-
stones, he came down gently from higher mountaintops to lower mountaintops until He descended on
Mount Sinai, as it says, *"Hashem came from Sinai; He
shone upon them from Seir; He appeared from Mount Paran.
From the holy myriads, He brought a law of fire to them
from His right Hand" (Devarim 33:2)*. This interpretation
is indisputable to anyone with an open mind.

Notice how unerringly accurate is the choice of
words in the text. Hashem's descent on Paran, which
is a more distant mountain, is described with the
vague term of *hofia*, "He appeared," while His emergence on Mount Seir which is closer, is characterized
with the more clear-cut verb *zarach*, "He shone."
Mount Sinai was His final destination, the place where
His glory came to rest. As we read, *"Hashem's glory rest-
ed on Mount Sinai" (Shemos 24:16)*. And so, with regard
to Mount Sinai we find the plainest and most explicit
phraseology, "Hashem **came** from Sinai."

It is noteworthy that Devorah portrays the Revelation on Mount Sinai in much the same way. She too,
is telling us that Hashem's glory came down gently
from mountain to mountain. Devorah expresses it this
way: *"Hashem, when You came forth from Seir, Advanced
from the country of Edom, The earth trembled; The heavens
dripped, Yea, the clouds dripped water" (Shofetim 5:4)*.

The Sages (Avodah Zarah 2b), offer a beautiful alle-
gorical interpretation of this verse. They say that ini-
tially, Hashem sent a messenger to the Edomites to

offer them the Torah, but they rejected it. Then He offered it to the Yishmaelites but they, too, rejected it. Finally, He sent Moshe Rabbeinu to us and we readily accepted the Torah, exclaiming, *"We will do and obey all that Hashem has declared"* (Shemos 24:7). Now all this took place **before** the Giving of the Torah, as is evident in the words "He came," "He shone" and "He appeared," which are all in the past tense, and do not presage future events.[3]

Discussion of Prophecy

There still remains the proof they derive from the passage, *"Hashem your God will raise up for you a prophet from among you, from your brothers,* kamoni—*like myself; him you shall obey" (Devarim 18:15).* In your letter you mention that [the word *kamoni*—like myself—in] this verse raised uncertainty in the minds of some of the people. [They claim that the Torah is foretelling the arrival of a prophet as great as Moshe]. Others cast off their doubts, as they realize that the Torah speaks of a prophet "from among you, from your brothers," [which Mohammed obviously is not]. [This leads me to believe that] were it not for the phrase *"from among you, from among your brothers,"* they would have considered this verse a valid proof. Please concentrate and pay very close attention to what I am about to tell you:

You must understand that you cannot simply take a word or a phrase out of context and use it to prove a

---

3. Whereas the Moslems falsely maintain that it alludes to Mohammed who was born almost 2,000 years after the Giving of the Torah.

point. You must consider the background clauses, both those that lead up to the statement and those that follow it. In other words, before using a fragment of a verse to bolster your argument, you must look at the entire verse and the paragraph in which that verse is found. Only then can you grasp the meaning of that phrase. Only then can you use that phrase to prove your hypothesis. A statement that is detached from its surrounding clauses cannot be advanced as proof. For if it were permissible to bring proof from passages taken out of context, you could say that Hashem has forbidden us to obey any prophet. After all, it is written, *"Do not heed the words of that prophet" (Devarim 13:4)*. What's more, [following this logic] you could say that Hashem commands us to worship idols—Hashem forbid—for it says in the Torah, *"You shall serve other Gods and bow to them" (Devarim 11:16)*. Many other such examples can be cited. This demonstrates the idiocy of such proofs and establishes the rule that you cannot adduce any proof whatsoever from a word or phrase unless you understand the context of that word.

Now, take the present verse, *"a prophet from among you, from your brothers, like myself."* Consider the context; *Let there not be found among you one who passes his son or daughter through fire, an augur, a soothsayer, a diviner, one who practices witchcraft, who uses incantations, who consults mediums and oracles, or who attempts to communicate with the dead (Devarim 18:10,11). You must be totally faithful to Hashem your God. The nations that you are driving out listen to astrologers and stick-diviners, but what Hashem has given you is totally different. Hashem your God will raise up for you a prophet from among you, from your brothers, like myself, and it is to him that you must listen (Devarim 18:13,15).*

The paragraph begins by warning us against becoming involved with sorcerers, soothsayers, and the like.

In other words, [don't involve yourselves] with people who perform occult practices by means of which the gentiles think they can predict future events. In warning us against engaging in such practices, Hashem tells us that the gentiles think that these procedures are effective in forecasting the future. But we should not use such means to ascertain what the future holds. We are to learn these things from a prophet whom He will raise up for us to inform us of what lies ahead. This prophet will foretell the future without resorting to sorcery, black magic, astrology or other occult practices.

The Torah goes on to tell us that finding out what the future holds will not require any effort on our part. Every prophet that Hashem will send us will come *from among you*. Thus, you will not have to travel great distances, journeying from town to town, before you can find him. Next, the Torah tells you another thing: in addition to being close to you and among you, he will also be one of your brothers. He will be a Jew. Therefore, the attribute of Divine prophecy will be restricted to the Jewish people. To emphasize this point the words *like myself*, have been added. You might mistakenly infer that *from your brothers*, also includes [a prophet who is a descendant] of Eisav or Yishmael. Such a mistake could easily be made. We do read that when Moshe sent envoys to the king of Edom [a descendant of Eisav] he addressed him as "brother," stating, *"Thus says your brother Yisrael . . ."* *(Bamidbar 20:14)*. To preclude this error it was necessary to add the clause, *"like myself,"* meaning "a Jew."

To contend that the phrase "like myself" implies that a prophet will arise who will be as great as Moshe is impossible, for we read, *"Never again did there arise in Yisrael a prophet like Moshe" (Devarim 34:10).*

The True and the False Prophet

It should be absolutely clear that the prophet who will arise will not issue any new commandments or create innovations in the Torah. He will not resort to occult practices, but we will be able to ask him about future events, the way the gentiles consult astrologers and fortunetellers. An example of this is when young Shaul went to ask the prophet Shmuel where he could find his father's donkeys that had gone astray *(Shmuel I 9:3-14)*.

The reason we do not believe the prophecies of Zeid and Amar is not because they are not Jewish. Many people have this erroneous idea because they infer this from the phrase, *"a prophet from among you, from your brothers."* After all, *Iyov* and his friends Tzofer, Bildad, Elifaz and Elihu received prophecy, even though they were not Jewish. On the other hand, Chananiah ben Azur a Jew, was a false prophet. A prophet should be believed because of what he preaches, not for reasons of lineage.

It is an established fact that Moshe Rabbeinu is the supreme prophet. When we heard the Divine Voice speak to him we believed in him and his prophecy. We said to him, *"You approach Hashem our God, and listen to all He says" (Devarim 8:24)*. Moshe told us that there are no commandments left in heaven to be given. There exists neither another faith nor another Torah beside the one we received. He said, *"It is not in heaven, so [that you should] say, "Who shall go up to heaven and bring it to us so that we can hear it and keep it?" (Devarim 30:12)*. He warned us neither to add nor to subtract from the Torah, saying, *"Do not add to it and do not subtract from it" (Devarim 13:1)*. Further, in Hashem's Name, he required us, our children and children's children, to believe in this Torah until the end of time. This is evident in the following verse, *"Hidden things concern Hashem our God, but that which has been revealed applies to us and our children forever. [We must therefore] keep all the words of the Torah (Devarim 29:28).*

If a prophet ever appears, regardless of his lineage, who says that one of the commandments of the Torah has been abrogated, he contradicts and denies what Moshe said: that the Torah applies "to us and our children forever." Therefore, we must denounce him. If we have the power to do so, we must put him to death. We must disregard any miracles he might perform, just as we pay no attention to a prophet who tells us to worship other gods. As we read, *"Even if the miracle or sign comes true, do not listen to the words of that prophet or dreamer" (Devarim 13:3,4).* Since Moshe told us never to worship other gods, we know with certainty that the "miracles" he performed in the name of the foreign deity are nothing but trickery and magic. Since Moshe told us explicitly that the Torah will last forever, we know that any prophet who claims that it is valid for only a set length of time is a false prophet. He is contradicting Moshe Rabbeinu. Consequently, we should not even ask him to corroborate his message through a sign or miracle. If he did perform a miracle we should ignore and dismiss it. We must realize that our belief in Moshe was not based on the miracles he performed. Therefore, we do not have to compare the miracles of this "prophet" to the miracles of Moshe. We believe in Moshe with complete, everlasting and unshakable trust because we heard the Revelation just as he heard it. This is expressed in the verse, *"They will believe in you forever" (Shemos 19:9).*

This makes us and Moshe like two witnesses who testify that they observed an event. Each witness knows with certainty that both his own and his part-

ner's testimony is true. No further proof of their veracity is needed.

The same is true in our case. We, the community of
Yisrael, were convinced of the trustworthiness of
Moshe Rabbeinu, because we ourselves were there
when Hashem spoke at Mount Sinai. When Moshe
performed miracles it was only because the situation
demanded it, as is evident from the Torah verses. This
important principle has been widely ignored and most
people do not rely on it any longer. Therefore, [it
should be reiterated that] our belief in Moshe Rabbeinu is far greater than our trust in miracles. Shlomoh
had this in mind when he wrote, *"Have you anything to
show like the encirclement of the two camps?" (Shir
Hashirim 4:1)*. In a figurative sense, Yisrael is saying to
the nation, "Can you show us anything as magnificent
as the Revelation on Sinai?"

Therefore, if a Jewish or even a non-Jewish prophet
urges people to follow the Jewish faith without adding
or subtracting from it, as Yeshayah, Yirmiyah and others like them did, we should demand that he perform
a miracle. If he does, we believe in him, and recognize
him as a prophet. But if he fails, and one of his predic-
tions remains unfulfilled, he must be put to death. We
believe him if he gives a sign, even though he might
be an impostor. Hashem told us in the Torah that if
two witnesses testify in a case, we bring in a verdict
on the basis of their testimony. Although we cannot
be absolutely sure their testimony is true, we give the
witnesses the benefit of the doubt and rely on their
reputation of honesty, even though we cannot be
absolutely sure whether their testimony is true. So
too, the Torah states, if a prophet predicts the future
or performs a miracle and his prediction comes true,
we accept him, even though we cannot say with certainty that he is a true prophet. At the same time, we

are told explicitly the major factor that disqualifies a prophet: if he says anything that contradicts the prophecy of Moshe Rabbeinu.

The entire subject of prophecy has been thoroughly and extensively discussed in our Introduction to the Commentary on the Mishnah[4]. There you will find a detailed analysis of this important principle that forms the cornerstone of the Torah and is the pillar of our faith. You should realize that not only is it forbidden to add to or subtract from the Torah, but even the Oral Law that was handed down by the Sages from one generation to the next may not be altered.

4. See Pages 6-23 in English translation by Avraham Yaakov Finkel, published by Yeshivah Beth Moshe of Scranton PA, 1993.

The Coming of Mashiach—
The Messiah

Calculations of the
Date of Redemption

Your letter mentions the calculations that *Rabbeinu Saadiah Gaon*[1] made for the date of the coming of Mashiach. You should be aware that no human being will ever be able to determine the exact date [of Mashiach's coming], as Daniel stated, *"For these words are secret and sealed to the time of the end" (Daniel 12:9).* Nevertheless, many theories were suggested by a few scholars who thought that they had discovered the date. This was predicted by Daniel, *"Many will run far*

---

1. Rabbeinu Saadiah Gaon (892–942 CE), one of the foremost personalities in Jewish history. He wrote Emunos Vedeyos (in Arabic), a seminal philosophical work.

and wide and opinions will increase" (Daniel 12:4). In other words, there will be much speculation about it. Furthermore, Hashem informed us through His prophets that many people will calculate the time of the coming of Mashiach; the date will pass and nothing will happen. We are warned against yielding to doubt and misgivings because of these miscalculations. We are urged not to be disillusioned if these computations do not come to fruition. We are told: The longer the delay, the more intensely you should hope. As it says, *"For there is yet a prophecy for a set term, it declares of the end and does not lie. Even if it tarries wait for it still; for it will surely come, without delay" (Chavakuk 2:3).*

Even the date of the end of the Egyptian exile was not exactly known, this gave rise to various interpretations. Hashem, however, clearly spelled it out, stating, *"They will be enslaved and oppressed for four hundred years"* (Bereishis 15:13). Some thought that the period of four hundred years began when Yaakov arrived in Egypt. Others counted it from the beginning of Yisrael's enslavement, which happened seventy years later. Others figured it from the time of the *Bris Bein Habesarim* (The Covenant of the Halves), when this prophecy was given to Avraham. As our sages taught us, four hundred years after this Covenant, and thirty years before Moshe appeared on the scene, a group of the Children of Yisrael [from the tribe of Ephraim] left Egypt. They thought that the predicted end of the exile had arrived. However, the Egyptians captured and killed them and increased the workload of the Hebrew slaves [who remained in Egypt]. David alluded to these men who miscalculated and left Egypt, in the verse, *"Like the Ephraimite bowmen who turned back in the day of battle" (Tehillim 78:9).*

The end of the Egyptian exile came four hundred years after the birth of Yitzchak the heir of Avraham, as it is written, *"It is through Yitzchak that you will gain posterity" (Bereishis 21:12)*. About him it was said, *"Your descendants will be foreigners in a land that is not theirs. They will be enslaved and oppressed for four hundred years" (Bereishis 15:13)*. During this exile, they would rule over them, enslave them and wear them down. The four hundred years refer only to exile and not to the years of enslavement. This was misunderstood until the great prophet (Moshe) came. When the Exodus took place exactly four hundred years after the birth of Yitzchak, it became clear. Now, if so much uncertainty surrounded the end of the Egyptian exile [the duration of which was known], then surely the end of this long exile is shrouded in obscurity. Its long duration has appalled and dismayed the prophets to the point that one of them exclaimed in utter amazement, *"Will You be angry with us forever, prolong Your wrath for all generations?" (Tehillim 85:6)*. Yeshayah, too, alluded to the seeming endlessness of this exile. He stated, *"They shall be gathered in a dungeon as prisoners are gathered; They shall be locked up in a prison. But after many days they shall be released" (Yeshayah 24:22)*.

Daniel declared the date of the final redemption a deep secret. Our Sages have discouraged the calculation of the time of the coming of Mashiach. They feared that the masses may be confused and led astray when the predicted time arrives and Mashiach does not come. This led our Sages to say, "May the people that calculate the final redemption meet with adversity" (Sanhedrin 97b).

Although making calculations of the time of redemption is forbidden we must judge Rabbeinu Saadiah Gaon favorably. The Jews of his time were influenced by many distorted ideologies. If not for [Rabbeinu Saadiah's] work of explaining the perplexing portions of the Torah and strengthening their faltering faith with the power of his word and his pen they would have abandoned the Torah altogether. He sincerely believed that by means of Messianic calculations he could rally the Jewish public, encourage them and inspire them with hope. Whatever he did was done for the sake of heaven. Since he had only the purest of motives we should not fault him for engaging in Messianic calculations.

The Rambam Rejects Astrology

I notice that you have a liking for astrology, and you find meaning in the constellations and conjunctions of planets. You should reject such thoughts and banish such concepts from your minds. Cleanse your mind of these worthless ideas like you wash dirt from your clothes. Accomplished non-Jewish scholars, and certainly Jewish scholars, do not consider astrology a genuine science. Its theories can easily be disproved by rational arguments, but this is not the place to go into them.

Before Moshe rose to prominence, the astrologers had unanimously predicted that the Jewish nation would never be released from slavery or attain its independence. Just when the astrologers thought the Jewish people had reached the bottom of degradation, destiny shone brightly on Yisrael. The most illustrious human being (Moshe) was born among them. Just when the astrologers unanimously foretold that Egypt would enjoy a period of wholesome climate, prosperity and tranquility, the plagues struck. Speaking of these failed forecasts, Yeshayah says, *"Where indeed are your sages? Let them tell you; let them discover what the God of Hosts has planned against Egypt" (Yeshayah 19:12).*

The same thing happened to the kingdom of Nebuchadnezzar. When all the astrologers, scholars and wise men unanimously agreed that his reign marked the beginning of a long period of supremacy, his empire collapsed and vanished from the scene. This was foretold by Hashem through Yeshayah. [Yeshayah] ridiculed their scholars and wise men who boasted of their wisdom. He mocked the government that took pride in its outstanding scholars. Said Yeshayah, *"You are helpless despite all your art. Let them stand up and help you now, the astrologers, the star-gazers, who announce, month by month, whatever will come upon you (Yeshayah 47:13).*

The same situation will prevail in the days of Mashiach, may he soon come. The gentiles believe that our people will never become an independent nation nor will they ever be released from the subservient condition they are in. All the astrologers and sorcerers will share this opinion. Hashem will give lie to their thoughts and discredit their false views by revealing the Mashiach. Yeshayah said this prophecy, *"[It is I] Who annuls the omens of diviners, and makes fools of the augurs; Who turns sages back, and makes nonsense of their knowledge; Who confirms the word of My servant, and fulfills the prediction of My messengers. It is I Who says of Jerusalem, 'It shall be inhabited,' and of the towns of Judah, 'They shall be rebuilt; and their ruins I will restore'"* (Yeshayah 44:25,26).

[Therefore,] do not pay any attention to astrological theories that deal with the conjunction of the stars in the greater or smaller constellations.

Disproves Astrologers' Allegations

You write that science is at a low ebb and research is non-existent in your country (Yemen). You attribute this to the influence of the constellations in the earthly trigon [of the zodiac][2]. Please understand that this lack of learning is prevalent not only in your country. Disrespect of sages and poor standards of education are widespread throughout Yisrael today. A Divine prophecy predicts this, stating, *"Truly, I shall further baffle that people with bafflement upon bafflement; and the wisdom of its wise shall fail, and the prudence of its prudent shall vanish" (Yeshayah 29:14).* This situation is not due to the earthly or the fiery trigon. This can be proved by the fact that King Shlomoh lived during the earthly trigon. Yet he is described as *"the wisest of all men" (Melachim I 8:11).* In the same way our Father, Avraham, who is called the Pillar of the World, discovered the First Cause of all Creation. He taught it to all the scholars, and proclaimed the fundamental principle of the Unity of God to all mankind. Furthermore, Avraham, Yitzchak and Yaakov carried the Throne of Glory in their hearts: they attained a true understanding of the Essence of the *Shechinah* (glory of Hashem). The Sages said, "The Patriarchs are the chariots [of the Shechinah]", which the Midrash (Bereishis Rabbah 82:7) derives from the verse, *"Hashem rose up from*

---

2. The zodiac is an imaginary belt encircling the heavens. It is divided into twelve parts, called signs of the zodiac or *mazalos* that correspond to twelve constellations bearing the same name (Aries, Taurus, Gemini etc. or in Hebrew, *T'leh, Shor, Te'omim, Sartan, Aryeh, Besulah, Moznayim, Akrov, Keshes, G'di, D'li, Dagim*). The zodiac is also divided into four quarters, called trigons, each consisting of three signs. The four trigons represent earth, water, air and fire. Astrologers believe that the influence of the earthly trigon causes a decrease in the pursuit of knowledge.

upon him" (Bereishis 35:13). Yet the three Patriarchs lived during the earthly trigon.

Let me explain. There is a small conjunction[3] in which Saturn and Jupiter come together. This happens once in about twenty solar years. This conjunction repeats itself 12 times in each trigon so that they conjunct in each trigon for 240 years. Then they move into the next trigon in what is called the medium conjunction. According to this calculation, an interval of nine hundred and sixty years will elapse between the first and second conjunction of two planets in the same point of the zodiac. This is called the great conjunction. It extends for nine hundred and sixty years, from the first until the second meeting of Saturn and Jupiter in the constellation Aries. By counting back, you will understand all that I have said about Avraham, Yitzchak and Yaakov, as well as David and Shlomoh living during the earthly trigon. My aim in explaining all this is to convince you to dismiss any thought you might have that the trigon can influence human affairs.

You also wrote that some people calculated that at some future point all seven planets will come together in one of the constellations of the zodiac. This just is not true. There will never be a meeting of the seven planets, neither in the next conjunction nor in any future ones. This calculation was made by an ignorant person, which is evident from another statement of his, that you quote, to the effect that there will be a flood of air and dust.

You must recognize that these and similar statements are nothing but lies and deceptions. Do not believe such things just because they are in a book;

3. In astronomy, conjunction means the position of two planets when they are in the same longitude.

the liar shrinks no more from deceiving with his pen than he does with his mouth. Fools and the uneducated will take a written statement at face value. But one must demand proof before he can believe a theory.

A blind person relies on a sighted man for direction and follows his guidance. A sick person will follow his doctor's orders and advice. It is essential for people at large to place their trust in the prophets who were men of true insight and rely on them when they are taught the truth or falsehood of a given teaching. In the absence of prophets [people should look for guidance] from the sages who study and analyze wisdom and doctrines day and night, and can distinguish between the truth and that which is false.

I want to impress on you that anything you heard or read on the subject of astrology and related fields is untrue. The author of such statements is either a fool, a clown or one who tries to destroy the Torah and tear down its protective walls. Don't you recognize the audacity of these individuals who say that there will be a flood of air and dust? They might as well say, there will be a deluge of fire. Their prediction is meant to mislead and seduce people into believing that the deluge in the time of Noach was caused merely by a convergence of water. They claim that it was not sent as a punishment by the True Judge for the many sins of the world's population, contrary to the teachings of the Torah. If you follow their reasoning, Sedom and the other cities, were not destroyed because of their lack of belief and the wickedness of their inhabitants. This is a direct denial of the Torah, which says, *"I will go down and see, if they have acted according to the outcry that has reached Me; I will destroy them" (Bereishis 18:21).* Whatever happens in the world by the Hand of Hashem, they say is the outcome of the conjunctions of the planets.

They advance these theories because they want to undermine the principles of our faith and unleash their animal lusts and cravings, like beasts and ostriches. Hashem warned us in the Torah against this view. He said that, "If you make Me angry you will be struck with disaster because of your transgressions. But if you attribute these disasters to chance rather than to your sinful conduct, then I will increase your calamities more and more". This is spelled out in the Chapter of Reproof, where it says, *"If you are* keri *to Me... then I will be-*keri *to you with a vengeance"* (Vayikra 26:27,28) The word *keri* means "something that is unplanned, that happens by chance; by accident." Thus the meaning of the verse is: "If you treat My acts as an accident...then I will increase this kind of 'accident' with a vengeance bringing yet another sevenfold increase in your punishment for your sins."

The above remarks make it abundantly clear that the coming of Mashiach is in no way influenced by the orbits of the stars.

It should be noted that one of the brilliant scholars in Andalusia, Spain, wrote a book, in which he calculated by means of astrology, the date of the final redemption and predicted the coming of Mashiach in a certain year. Every one of our pious scholars sneered at his words, belittled his scheme and ostracized him for what he had done in foretelling the future. But reality dealt him a more severe blow than we could have. At the very time Mashiach was supposed to make his appearance [by his reckoning], a rebel leader rose up in the Maghreb who issued an order for everyone to convert. The rebel takeover ruined the reputation of the practitioners of astrology. The hardships our people suffered in the Exile caused them to turn to pseudo-sciences that do not have a shred of evidence to back them up.

Words of Encouragement

Now, dear brothers, *"be strong and of good courage, all you who wait for Hashem" (Tehillim 31:25)*. Strengthen one another. Implant in everyone's heart the faith in the coming of the Redeemer, may he soon appear. *"Strengthen the hands that are slack and make firm tottering knees" (Yeshayah 35:3)*. Remember, Hashem has let us know through Yeshayah, the herald of Yisrael, that the prolonged affliction of the exile will lead many people to believe that He has abandoned us and turned away from us—God forbid. In light of that, He assured us that He will never abandon us or forget us. As it says, *"Zion says, 'Hashem has forsaken me, Hashem has forgotten me.'"* The prophecy continues, *"Can a woman forget her baby, or disown the child of her womb? Though she might forget, I never could forget you" (Yeshayah 49:14,15)*. Hashem has already related a similar message through the first prophet (Moshe), stating, *"For Hashem your God is a compassionate God. He will not fail you nor will He let you perish; He will not forget the covenant with the fathers which He swore to them" (Devarim 4:31)*, Also, *"Hashem will bring back your remnants and have mercy on you. Hashem your God will once again gather you from among all the nations where He scattered you" (Devarim 30:3)*.

Dear brothers, it is one of the cornerstones of the Jewish faith that a Redeemer will arise who is a descendant of Shlomoh. He will gather in our scattered ones, take away our humiliation, publicize the true religion and wipe out those who flout His commands. Hashem promised this in the Torah. *"I see it, but not now; I perceive it, but not in the near future. A star[4] shall go forth from Yaakov, and a staff shall arise in Yisrael, crushing*

---

4.   This is a messianic prophecy.

all of Moab's princes, and dominating all of Shes's descendants. Edom shall be demolished, and his enemy Seir destroyed, but Yisrael shall be triumphant" (Bamidbar 24:17,18). The time of his arrival will be a period of great calamity for the Jewish people. As it is written, *"He will have seen that their power is gone, and none is left to set free or take captive"* (Devarim 32:36). Only then Hashem will identify Mashiach, and He will fulfill the promises He made. The prophet, horrified by the vision of the time the Redeemer will appear, exclaimed, *"Who can endure the day of his coming, and who can hold out when he appears?"* (Malachi 3:2). This is the correct view that you must believe about this subject.

We know from the prophecies of Daniel and Yeshayah, and from the words of our Sages, that Mashiach will come after the Roman and Arab empires have swept across the world. This is the case today. No one can doubt this or deny it. Only after Daniel spoke of the Arab empire and the rise of Mohammed, did he speak of the coming of Mashiach which will take place afterward. Yeshayah, too, declared in his vision, that the arrival of Mashiach is linked to the appearance of the Madman (Mohammed). He says, *"He will see mounted men, horsemen in pairs, riders on donkeys, riders on camels, and he will listen closely, most attentively"* (Yeshayah 21:7). Now the rider on the donkey is Mashiach who is described as *"humble, riding on a donkey"* (Zechariah 9:9). He will come soon after the rise of the man riding a camel. That is, the Arab empire. The phrase "horsemen in pairs" refers to the bond between the two empires Edom and Yishmael. The same interpretation applies to Daniel's dream of the statue and the beasts[5]. You can plainly see this by simply reading the verses.

5.   The Rambam is referring to Daniel, chapters 2 and 7.

The Rambam's Amazing Family Tradition

The exact date of the coming of Mashiach cannot be known. But I have in my possession a great and amazing tradition which I received from my father. He received it from his father and his grandfather, going back to our ancestors who went into exile at the time of the destruction of Jerusalem. As it says, *"and the exiles of Jerusalem that are in Spain"* (Ovadiah 1:20).

This tradition is that *Bilam's* sayings contain a hint of the future restoration of prophecy in Yisrael. There are many instances where a verse in the Torah, in addition to its simple meaning, also contains an allusion to something else. For example, we find that Yaakov, speaking to his sons, said, "R'du—*Go down there [to Egypt]*" (Bereishis 42:2). *R'du* has the numeric value of 210 which is an allusion to the 210 years the children of Yisrael would be exiled in Egypt. So too, *venoshantem*, in the verse, *"When you have children and grandchildren,* venoshantem—*and have been established for a long time in the land"* (Devarim 4:25), foretells in a hidden way how long the Jewish people would live in Eretz Yisrael. From the time they entered the land until the exile in the days of King Yehoyakim is a total of 840 years. This is the numeric value of *venoshantem*. Many similar examples can be cited.

The family tradition which I received is based on this system of scriptural interpretation [by means of *remez*—hidden allusion]. The tradition is based on Bilam's oracle, "Ka'eis—*at this point in time—it is said of Yaakov and of Yisrael: 'What God is doing'"* (Bamidbar 23:23). This contains a concealed allusion regarding the restoration of prophecy in Yisrael. [Based on another

translation of *ka'eis,* which means "equal to the time"]
the verse means that after the passage of a period
equal to the time that elapsed since the six days of
Creation, prophecy would be restored in Yisrael.
Prophets will once again foretell *"what God is doing".*
Bilam made this prediction in the fortieth year after
the Exodus, which was the year 2488 of Creation.
According to this equation, prophecy will be restored
in Yisrael in the year 4976[6] of Creation. It is true beyond doubt that the restoration of prophecy is the first
phase of the coming of Mashiach. As it is stated, *"After
that I will pour out My spirit on all flesh; your sons and
daughters shall prophesy" (Yoel 3:1).*

This is the most dependable of all the calculations
that have been made about the coming of Mashiach.
Although I have spoken out against making such
calculations and strongly opposed the publicizing of
the date of his arrival, I have done this in order to
keep people from [falling into despair], thinking that
his coming is in the distant future. I have mentioned
this to you earlier. Blessed is Hashem Who knows [the
truth].

You mention in your letter that ours is the time [of
the coming of Mashiach] about which Yirmiyah
prophesied, *"It is a time of trouble for Yaakov, but he shall
be delivered from it" (Yirmiyah 30:7).* This is not correct.
This verse definitely refers to the wars of Gog and
Magog, which will take place some time after the
appearance of Mashiach.

The various signs you mention are very flimsy. They
are not attributed to our Sages and were not given by
them. Some of them are proverbs and allegories that
have nothing to do with this subject.

6. Two times 2488 equals 4976. The year 4976 of Creation corresponds
    with 1216 C.E. It should be remembered that the Rambam wrote the
    Letter to Yemen in 1172.

The False Mashiach

You write about a certain man who makes the rounds of the cities of Yemen, claiming to be Mashiach. Let me assure you that I am not surprised at him. Without a doubt, the man is insane. You cannot blame a sick person for an illness that is not his own doing. Neither am I shocked at the masses who believe in him. They were captivated by him due to their broken spirit and their ignorance of both the illustrious character of Mashiach and the place where he will appear. However, I am astonished that you, a Torah scholar who is well-versed in the Talmud and its commentaries, came under his spell. Don't you know, dear brother, that Mashiach is a prophet of the highest order who ranks higher than any other prophet with the exception of Moshe Rabbeinu? Don't you know that a person who falsely pretends to be a prophet must be put to death for having assumed this great title, just as a person who prophesied in the name of idols must be executed? The Torah states, *"If a prophet presumptuously makes a declaration in My name when I have not commanded him to do so, or if he speaks in the name of other gods, then that prophet shall die"* (Devarim 18:20). What stronger proof is there that he is a liar than his laying claim to the title of Mashiach?

I am really puzzled by your remark about this man; that he is known to be a serene person who has some wisdom. Do you really think these qualities make him Mashiach? You were convinced by him because you have not given any thought to the grandeur of Mashiach, nor to how and where he would appear, and by what specific sign he can be identified. Mashiach will be more sublime and more revered than any other prophet, except *Moshe Rabbeinu*. The marks of distinction Hashem has given him are even greater than those of Moshe Rabbeinu. Mashiach is described in the following terms: *"His delight shall be in the fear of God; he shall not judge by what his eyes behold, nor decide by what his ears perceive" (Yeshayah 11:3)*, and *"The spirit of God shall rest upon him: a spirit of wisdom and insight, a spirit of counsel and valor, a spirit of devotion and reverence for God" (Yeshayah 11:2)*. *"Justice shall be the girdle of his loins and faithfulness the girdle of his waist" (Yeshayah 11:5)*. Hashem called him six special names in this verse: *"For a child has been born to us, a son has been given us, and authority has settled on his shoulders. He has been named Wondrous One, Adviser, Great, Strong, Eternal Father, Peaceable Ruler" (Yeshayah 9:5)*. The name Great is meant as a superlative: to tell you that he is superior to any human being.

We know that one of the basic conditions for a prophet is that he posses limitless knowledge and wisdom. Only to such an individual will Hashem grant the power of prophecy. It is a fundamental belief that prophecy is granted only to a man who is wise, strong and wealthy. The Sages explain that strong means the ability to subdue one's cravings. Wealthy means rich in knowledge. If we do not believe a man's claim to prophecy unless he is a scholar of eminent stature, then surely we must not believe an ignoramus who claims that he is Mashiach. This person is an illiterate know-nothing. This is apparent from the command he issued to the people to donate all their money to the poor. Whoever obeyed him is a fool, for this man acted against the laws of the Torah. According to the Torah, one should give away only part of his money to charity, not all of it. It says, *"But of all that anyone owns, be it man or beast or land of his holding, nothing that he has consecrated for Hashem may be sold or redeemed" (Vayikra 27:28)*. The Sages of the Talmud interpret the phrase "**of** all that anyone owns" to mean, "part of what he owns, but not all that he owns". Based on this passage, they placed a limit on how much you should give to charity. They stated, "Whoever wants to be liberal should not give away more than one fifth of his possessions" (Kesuvos 50a). No doubt, the same insanity that motivated this man to claim that he is Mashiach prompted him to order his followers to give all their possessions to the needy. As a result, the rich will become poor and the poor will become rich. By his law, the newly rich then would have to return the money they received to the newly needy. The money would then move around in a vicious cycle, which is the height of stupidity.

Characteristics of the True Mashiach

Regarding the question of how and where Mashiach will appear; we know he will make his first appearance in Eretz Yisrael. As it says, *"Suddenly he will come to His temple" (Malachi 3:1)*. But no one will know how he will arise until it actually happens. Mashiach will not be a

known person that can be identified beforehand as the
son of so-and-so of such-and-such family. The signs
and wonders he will perform will be proof that he is
the true Mashiach. We are told by Hashem regarding
Mashiach's person, *"Behold, a man called Tzemach
(Sprout) shall sprout forth from the place where he is"
(Zechariah 6:12)*. Similarly, Yeshayah said that he will
arrive without anyone knowing anything about either
his father, mother or family: *"For he shot up like a
sapling, like a root out of dry ground" (Yeshayah 53:2)*.

After making his appearance in Eretz Yisrael and
gathering the entire Jewish people in Jerusalem and
the surrounding countryside, the news will spread to
the East and the West until it reaches Yemen and the
Jews beyond in India. This has been prophesied by
Yeshayah, *"Go, swift messengers to a nation tall and of
glossy skin, to a people awesome from their beginning
onward; a nation that is sturdy and treads down, whose land
rivers divide . . . To the place where the name of Hashem of
Hosts abides, to Mount Zion" (Yeshayah 18:2,7)*.

The qualities of Mashiach are described by all the
prophets from Moshe to *Malachi*. You can gather this
information from the twenty-four books of *Tanach*. His
most outstanding characteristic is that the news of his
coming will appall and terrify all the kings of the
world. Their kingdoms will collapse. Their attempts to
defy him by military force or otherwise will utterly
fail. Overwhelmed by the miracles they are witness-
ing, they will stare openmouthed at the wonders he
performs. Yeshayah portrays the subservience of the
kings to Mashiach in the verse, *"Kings will be silenced
because of him, for they will see what has not been told them,
will behold what they never have heard" (Yeshayah 52:15)*.
He will kill whomever he wants by word of his
mouth. No one can escape or be saved, as it says, *"He
will strike down a land with the rod of his mouth, and slay*

the wicked with the breath of his lips" (Yeshayah 11:4).
Worldwide upheavals and wars, ranging from East to
West will not come to an end at the beginning of the
reign of Mashiach, but only after the wars of Gog and
Magog. This was foretold by Yechezkel *(Yechezkel
38,39).*

The False Mashiach is Insane

I do not believe that the man who has appeared in
your country has any of these qualifications. The
Christians falsely attribute great miracles to *oso ha'ish*—
"that man" (the founder of their religion), such as re-
viving the dead. Even if we conceded this for the sake
of argument, we could not accept their argument that
Jeshu is Mashiach. We can show them a thousand
proofs in *Tanach* that he is not, even from their point of
view. Indeed, would anyone lay claim to this title
unless he wanted to make himself a laughingstock?

To summarize, if this man had made his claim willfully and scornfully, he would deserve to die a thousand times. I tend to believe that he became mentally
unbalanced and lost his mind. Let me offer you advice
that will benefit both you and him: Lock him up until
the gentiles find out about it, and pass the word
around that he is crazy. Afterwards you can release
him, and he will be safe. For if the gentiles hear that
you locked him up because he claims to be Mashiach,
they will realize that you believe him insane, and you
will escape the anger of the gentiles. But if you delay
until the gentiles find out about it by themselves, they
will believe that he is trying to rebel. They will kill

him, and you might provoke their anger against your community, God forbid.

Submit to Oppression

Dear brothers, because of our many sins Hashem has cast us among this nation, the Arabs, who are treating us badly. They pass laws designed to cause us distress and make us despised. The Torah foretold: *"Our enemies will judge us" (Devarim 32:31)*. Never has there been a nation that hated, humiliated and loathed us as much as this one. So bad is our lot that when David had a Divinely inspired vision of the troubles that would happen to Yisrael, he bemoaned and lamented the suffering of the Jewish nation at the hands of the Arabs. He prayed on their behalf, saying, *"Woe is me, that I live with Meshech, that I dwell among the clans of Kedar" (Tehillim 120:5)*. Note how the verse sets apart Kedar from the other children of Yishmael. This is done because as everyone knows, the Madman is a descendant of the people of Kedar. Daniel, too, when speaking of our degradation and poverty associated with the Arab empire, may it soon be defeated, said, *"It hurled some stars of the [heavenly] host to the ground and trampled them" (Daniel 8:10)*. We suffered unbearable oppression and had to endure their lies and defamations. Yet, we acted like David as he describes himself in the verse, *"But I am like a deaf man, who does not hear, like a dumb man who does not open his mouth" (Tehillim 38:14)*. We followed the admonition of our Sages who told us to bear the deceit and the falsehood of Yishmael in silence. They found an allusion for this attitude in the names of Yishamel's sons, *"Mishma, Dumah and Massa" (Bereishis 25:14)*. They homiletically interpreted these names to mean, "Listen *(sh'ma)*, be silent *(dom)* and endure *(massa)"*. All of us, both old and young, agreed to put up with their tyranny. As Yeshayah told us, *"I offered my back to the floggers, and my cheeks to those who tore out my hair; I did not hide my face from insult and spittle" (Yeshayah 50:6)*. In spite of that, we cannot escape their constant abuse and harassment. Much as we try to appease them, they continue to persecute and molest us. As David said, *"I am all peace, but when I speak, they are for war" (Tehillim 120:7)*. Surely, if we stir up trouble and challenge the government with unfounded allegations we endanger ourselves and risk our lives.

Other Impostors

I want to tell you that when the Moslem empire began to rise[1], a man appeared on the other side of the river who pretended to be Mashiach. As proof, he performed a "miracle" by going to sleep afflicted with leprosy and waking up healthy. He inspired an exodus of tens of thousands of Jews. But his mission ended in failure and his plans collapsed. His followers returned to Ishfahan[2] and the Jews of Ishfahan suffered troubles because of him.

A similar incident occurred forty-eight years ago in

---

1. The religion of Islam was established in 622 C.E.
2. Ishfahan is a city in west central Iran, former capital of Persia.

the Maghreb, in the city of Fez[3]. A person declared himself the herald and messenger of Mashiach. He announced that Mashiach himself would arrive that very year. His prediction did not materialize, and the result was renewed persecutions of the Jews. I heard this from a person who was there and witnessed the entire episode.

About ten years before this incident[4], a man in Cordova, Spain claimed to be Mashiach. This brought that Jewish community to the brink of destruction.

Thirty years before his emergence[5], a man in France pretended to be Mashiach and performed so-called miracles. But the French killed him, and along with him they slew many in the Jewish community.

[The text of the above accounts of the emergence and fall of various impostors is found in the standard translations of the Iggeres Teiman from the Arabic by R. Shmuel ibn Tibbon, R. Nachum Maghrabi and R. Avraham Halevi ben Chasdai of Barcelona. The Rambam's original Arabic text is said to contain a much more detailed version of these reports. This original, full Arabic text has been translated into Hebrew by Dr. Jacob Mann in 1928.]

I will now briefly tell you the events that happened at the beginning of the rise of the Arab empire, which will be helpful to you. In one of these episodes, tens of thousands of Jews marched from the East beyond Isfahan, led by a man who pretended to be Mashiach[6]. They were carrying weapons and

---

3. Fez is a city in North East Morocco. This incident happened in 1127, forty-five years before the Rambam wrote the Iggeres Teiman in 1172.
4. In 1117.
5. In 1087.
6. The Rambam is referring to the false Mashiach Abu Isi Ovadiah from Isfahan, Persia who lived during the reign of Caliph Abd al Malach (659-705)

drawn swords. They killed everyone who tried to stop them. They ultimately reached the vicinity of Baghdad. This happened in the beginning of the reign of the Omayyad dynasty[7].

The Sultan then said to the Jews of his kingdom, "Let your rabbis go out to this crowd and determine whether he is indeed the one you are anticipating (Mashiach). If so, we will make a peace treaty with you and abide by any conditions you may set. But if it is untrue, I will kill them." When the rabbis met these Jews, they were told, "We come from the other side of the river." Then the rabbis asked them, "Who incited you to make this revolution?" They replied, "This man here, a descendant of David, whom we know to be a pious and upright man. We found out that he went to sleep a leper and arose the next morning cured and healthy." They thought this was one of the characteristics of Mashiach that is alluded to in the verse, *"plagued, smitten and afflicted by Hashem" (Yeshayah 53:4)*. The rabbis explained to them that this interpretation was wrong, and that he lacked many, if not all, of the qualities of Mashiach. The rabbis told them, "Brothers, since you are still close to your homeland, you can go back. If you stay here, you will perish. You will also invalidate the words of Moshe by misleading the people into thinking that Mashiach has appeared and has been vanquished. The truth is that there is no prophet among you, nor do you have a sign to substantiate your leader's claims." In the end, the Jews were convinced by the rabbis. The Sultan gave them a gift of thousands of dinars to induce them to return home. But after they had returned home, he imposed a fine on them to recover the vast amount of money he had given to them. He began to harass them. He ordered them to mark their clothing with the word "cursed," and to attach an iron bar to their backs and one to their chests. Ever since, the communities of Khorasan and Isfahan suffered the trials of the harsh exile. Report of this incident came to me by word of mouth.

The following episode I researched. I can vouch for its authenticity, because it happened not long ago. About fifty

---

7. The Omayyad dynasty ruled the Islamic empire from 661 to 750. They spread Islam over a large region.

years ago[8], Rabbi Moshe Dar'i, a pious and upright man, an
outstanding Torah scholar came from Dara[9] to Andalusia to
study under Rabbi Yosef Halevi Ibn Migash[10] of whom you
surely have heard. Later he left for Fez, in the center of the
Maghreb. People flocked to him because of his piety, his virtue
and his learning. He told them that Mashiach had come, and
that Hashem had revealed this to him in a dream. He did not
pretend to be Mashiach, as this lunatic did, he only declared
that Mashiach had already appeared. Many people became his
followers and believed him implicitly. My father and master
admonished the people not to follow him, and ordered them
to leave him. Only a few obeyed my father. Most, or to be
exact, almost all of them, remained faithful to Rabbi Moshe.
Finally, he foretold things that actually came true. He would
say to the crowd, "Tomorrow such will happen," and it did
happen precisely as he predicted. Once he predicted a heavy
rain for the coming week, and that the raindrops would be
blood. This was thought to be a sign of the coming of
Mashiach, as indicated in the verse, *"I will set portents in the
sky and on earth, blood and fire and pillars of smoke" (Yoel
3:3)*. This took place in the month of Marcheshvan. A very
heavy rain did indeed fall during that week. The raindrops
were reddish and muddy, as if mixed with clay. This miracle
proved to everyone that he was undoubtedly a prophet. This
occurrence is not inconsistent with the doctrine of the Torah.
Prophecy, as I explained, will return to Yisrael before the coming of Mashiach.

After the majority of the people had faith in him, he foretold
that Mashiach would come that same year, on the night of
Pesach. He advised the people to sell their property and buy
things on credit from the Moslems, paying ten dinars for something that is worth one. This they did. Pesach came and noth-

---

8. In 1122, fifty years before the Rambam wrote Iggeres Teiman in 1172.
9. Dara is a town in Morocco.
10. Rabbi Yosef Halevi ibn Migash, known as Ri Migash (1077-1141). He
    studied under the Rif (Rabbi Yitzchak Alfasi) and became his successor.
    As rosh yeshivah of Lucena, Spain, Rabbi Yosef taught Rabbi Maimon,
    father of the Rambam.

ing happened. The people were impoverished, since most of them had sold their possessions very cheaply, and were heavily burdened by debt. The gentiles and their slaves would have killed him (Rabbi Moshe Dar'i) were they able to find him. Since this Moslem country no longer offered him shelter, he left for Eretz Yisrael where he died, may his memory be blessed[11]. I was told by eyewitnesses that when he left [the Maghreb] he predicted both important and trivial things that actually happened later to the Jews of the Maghreb.

My father told me that about fifteen or twenty years before this incident[12], some respectable people in Cordova[13], the capital of Andalusia, who believed in astrology came to the conclusion that Mashiach would arrive that year. They sought a revelation in a dream, night after night, in order to find out whether Mashiach would be a native of their region. In the end, they chose a pious and virtuous person named Ibn Aryeh who had been teaching the people. He performed miracles and foretold the future, just as Al Dari did, until he won over the hearts of the people. When the elders and the rabbis of our community heard this, they assembled in the synagogue and had Ibn Aryeh brought there. They flogged him and imposed a fine on him. They also put him under a ban because he stood idly by and permitted people to use his name. He should have restrained them and reprimanded them for transgressing Torah law. They did the same thing to his followers. It was only with great difficulty that the Jews were saved from the gentiles.

About forty years before the incident of Ibn Aryeh in Andalusia, a man of Linon[14], a large city in France with a Jew-

11. Rabbi Moshe Dar'i was held in high regard when he moved to Eretz Yisrael after this incident. The Rambam mentions him respectfully in one of his responsa (Kovetz, Volume 1:26).
12. Sometime between 1102 and 1107.
13. Rabbi Maimon, the Rambam's father lived in Cordova with his family. When the Rambam was thirteen years old, the city fell to the fanatical Almohad Moslem sect. The family wandered from place to place for almost twelve years, and finally settled in Cairo, Egypt.
14. Presumably this is Lyons, France.

ish population numbering tens of thousands of families, proclaimed himself Mashiach. On a clear night, he went out into
the field, climbed to the top of a high tree and skipped and
jumped from tree to tree as though he were sailing through
the sky. He claimed that, according to Daniel, this feat proved
that he was Mashiach, as it says, *"One like a human being
came with the clouds of heaven, and he was given dominion,
glory, and a kingdom" (Daniel 7:13,14).*

The large crowd which witnessed the miracle became his
devoted followers. When the French found out about it they
pillaged the city and slew the imposter together with many of
his followers. Some of his adherents believe, however, that he
is hiding somewhere until this very day.

[End of translation of the detailed account that is omitted in
the standard translations, but appears in the original Arabic
text.]

Conclusion

These incidents[15] were predicted by our prophets.
They informed us, as I have told you, that when the
time of the coming of the true Mashiach approaches,
the number of people who pretend to be Mashiach
will increase. Their claims will not be substantiated
nor will they be borne out. They will perish and so
will many of their followers. Shlomoh was inspired by
ruach hakodesh (Divine spirit). He foresaw that the long
duration of the exile would induce some of our people
to take action to end it before the time of redemption
comes. As a result, they would perish or meet with
disaster. He, therefore, admonished the Jewish people

---

15. Of false messiahs arising in various places at various times.

against taking matters into their own hands. He put them under oath, stating, in a figurative sense, *"I adjure you, O maidens of Yerushalayim, by the gazelles or by the hinds of the field: Do not wake or rouse love until it is desired!" (Shir Hashirim 3:5)*. Now, dear brothers and friends, accept this oath upon yourselves and do not arouse love until it is desired.

May Hashem Who created the world with the attribute of Mercy remember us and gather us when He gathers in the dispersed of His exile to the Land of His Inheritance. Then may we behold the sweetness of Hashem and contemplate in His Sanctuary. May He take us out from the Valley of the Shadow of Death into which He has placed us. May He remove darkness from our eyes and gloom from our hearts. May He fulfill in our days and in your days the prophecy, *"The people that walked in darkness have seen a brilliant light, on those who dwelt in a land of gloom, light has dawned" (Yeshayah 9:1)*. May He in His fury spread darkness on all our oppressors. May He illuminate our pitch-blackness, as He promised us, *"Behold! Darkness shall cover the earth, and thick clouds the nations; but upon you Hashem will shine, and His Glory be seen over you" (Yeshayah 60:2)*.

Epilogue

Greetings to you, my dear friend, master of the sciences, storehouse of wisdom,[1] to all our learned colleagues, and to all the people of the country (Yemen). May there be peace as the light that shines; an abundance of peace until the moon is no more. Amen.

I request that you send a copy of this letter to every community, to its rabbis and members, to strengthen their faith and make them stand staunch and steadfast. Read it privately and at public gatherings. Thereby, you will lead the many to righteousness. Be extremely careful and cautious lest its contents fall into the hands of an evil person who would publicize them to the Moslems. This would bring misfortune in its wake, may Hashem in His mercy spare us from it. When I was writing the letter, I was very afraid of that. However, I realized that the mitzvah of leading the many to righteousness is something that one should not fear. In addition, I am sending this letter as a, *"secret of Hashem to those who fear Him[2]" (Tehillim 25:14).* Besides, the Sages gave us an assurance, which they in turn received from the prophets "persons engaged in doing a mitzvah will not suffer harm"(Pesachim 8a). Certainly, there is no mitzvah that is more important than this.

Peace upon all Yisrael. Amen.

---

1. This is Rabbi Yaakov al-Fayumi who was a learned rosh yeshivah in Yemen. The final paragraphs were written in Hebrew by the Rambam.
2. In other words, since you are a God-fearing man you will guard the letter and treat it discreetly.

Maamar Kiddush Hashem
Discourse On Martyrdom

Preface

The Letter on Martyrdom is a response by the Ram-bam to a query he received from a Jew in North Africa. The Jews of that region were forced to convert to Islam by the ruling Almohad Moslem sect, the same regime that had forced the Rambam to leave Spain and find refuge in Cairo. The questioner, a forced convert, asked a rabbi whether he should secretly observe as many *mitzvos* as he could. The rabbi ruled that any *mitzvah* a converted Jew performed, or any prayer he uttered, would constitute a sinful act. Shocked by the incorrectness of this answer, the Rambam wrote his Letter on Martyrdom. In it he ridiculed the rabbi's blatant misinterpretation of the law and offered instruction and counsel on the proper course to follow when confronted with religious coercion. This letter is much more than a response to one individual caught in a difficult situation. It is a timeless document that has provided guidance and succor during the countless persecutions and forced conversions the Jewish people have endured in our long exile.

Iggeres Teiman and Maamar Kiddush Hashem are two classic examples of the Rambam's illustrious greatness and his deep love of the Jewish people. The Rambam's total personality emerges in his Letters. The reader marvels at his humility, his kindness, and his wit. He smiles at the biting sarcasm with which he deflates false messiahs, pompous ignoramuses posing as rabbis, and assorted perverters of the truth. Like *Moshe Rabbeinu*, the Rambam winces at the pain each Jew is suffering. With deep compassion, he does his utmost to alleviate our torment. Like a father, he gently soothes our pain, encourages us and inspires us with hope and a sense of pride. Through the clarity of his writing the Rambam springs to life, exuding such warmth that one is spellbound by his words.

Not surprising, the Rambam is one of the most beloved and respected figures in Jewish history. His writings certainly confirm the famous aphorism inscribed on his tombstone, "From Moshe [Rabbeinu] till Moshe (the Rambam) none arose like Moshe."

Maamar Kiddush Hashem

A Misleading Answer

A contemporary of mine inquired about how he should act during these times of persecution[1], in which he is forced to acknowledge "that man[2]" [Mohammed] as G-d's messenger and a true prophet. He directed his question at someone whom he calls a sage and who [himself] was not affected by the persecutions that wreaked havoc on many of the Jewish com-

---

1. The Almohads, a fanatical Moslem sect which rose to power in Morocco and Spain(1130-1223), forced the Jewish population of these regions to choose between Islam and exile.
2. The Rambam is very reluctant to mention the name of the founder of Islam. Here he uses the term *oso ish*, "that man," the same expression used in referring to the founder of Christianity. In Iggeres Teiman he uses the appellation *hameshuga* - the madman, instead of *oso ish*.

munities, may Hashem end them soon. He asked whether he should make the confession in order to save his life; and that he be able to raise his children so that they will not be lost among the gentiles. Or, does the Torah of Moshe demand that he die and not accept their creed. We must also take into consideration that this confession may eventually cause him to abandon the observance of all the mitzvos.

The man whom he asked his question gave a weak and pointless answer, a reply that was repulsive both in meaning and language. He made statements that are utterly meaningless, as even unlearned women can realize.

Although his reply is long-winded, weak and tedious, I thought I would respond to his every point. However, I took pity on the gift Hashem bestowed on us, by that I mean [the power of] speech, as it says in the Torah, *"Who gives man speech? . . . Is it not I, Hashem?"* One should use words more sparingly than money. Indeed, the Wise Man (Shlomoh) has denounced [people who] talk much and say things of little substance, stating, *"Just as dreams come with much brooding, so does a fool's voice come with much speech"* *(Koheles 5:2)*. In the same way, you see what Iyov's friends said when he talked on and on, *"Is a multitude of words unanswerable? Must a talkative person be right?"* *(Iyov 11:2)*, *"Iyov does not speak with knowledge; his words lack understanding"* *(Iyov 34:35)*. Many other examples can be cited.

Since I am thoroughly familiar with this situation[3], and I do not want to burden you with the ignorance

---

3.   When the Rambam was thirteen years old, his father and the entire family fled Cordova after the city fell to the Almohads. They wandered from place to place for about twelve years, until they settled in Cairo, in 1165.

of this man, I think it is worthwhile to mention the thrust of what he said and omit that which does not deserve an answer. Although, on reflection, nothing he said is worthy of a reply.

He states at the outset that whoever acknowledges that [Mohammed] is a [divine] messenger has thereby automatically renounced his belief in Hashem, the God of Yisrael. He proves his assertion by citing the saying of our Sages, "Whoever acknowledges idolatry is considered as if he denied the entire Torah" (*Nedarim 28a*). In making this analogy he does not differentiate between a person who voluntarily accepts idolatry, like *Yerovam* and his clique, and one who says under duress that someone is a prophet, because he fears death by the sword.

When I read this first statement of his, I said to myself,"It is not right for me to attack him before reading all he has to say, in compliance with the words of Shlomoh, *"To answer a man before hearing him out is foolish and disgraceful" (Koheles 18:13)*.

When I scanned his words a bit more, I noticed that he said the following, "Whoever makes this confession is a gentile, even if he observes the entire Torah privately and publicly." Evidently, this "intelligent" individual [who does not differentiate between one who confessed voluntarily and one who confessed under duress] sees no difference between a person who does not observe Shabbos because he is afraid of the sword and one who does not observe it because he does not want to.

Then I read, "If one of the forced converts enters one of their houses of worship, even if he does not utter a word, and then goes home and says his prayer there, this prayer counts as an added sin and transgression." He brings proof from the comments of our Sages on the verse, *"For My people have done a twofold wrong" (Yirmiyah 2:13)* [which the Sages explain to mean,] "they bowed to the idol and then bowed to the *Beis Hamikdash" (Shir Hashirim Rabbah 1:6)*. This [would-be] "Bible commentator" makes no distinction between a heretic who willingly bowed to an idol and then in order to defile the *Bais Hamikdash* bowed to it, and one who enters a mosque under duress, pretends to promote the magnificence of their God, and does not utter a single word opposed to our religion.

Likewise, he said that "Whoever acknowledges that this man [Mohammed] is a prophet, although compelled to do so, is a wicked person and is disqualified by the Torah from serving as a witness, as it says, *"Do not join forces with a wicked person to be a corrupt witness" (Shemos 23:1)*, [which the Talmud expounds to mean], "do not make a wicked man a witness"*(Bava Kamma 72b)*.

Even as I read his blasphemous insults and his inane and foolish long-winded chatter, I said to myself, it still is not right to criticize him before I read the rest of his writing. It might be as Shlomoh said, *"The end of a matter is better than the beginning of it" (Koheles 7:8)*.

However the end of his discourse says "Even heretics and Christians would choose death rather than acknowledge that [Mohammed] has divine mission." When I read this I was utterly shocked and amazed I wondered, *"Is there no God in Yisrael" (Melachim II 1,3)*. ["Do the Jewish people lack their own laws? Can we derive the proper way to act from the gentiles?"]. If an idol worshiper burns his son or his daughter to his idol, should we say that we too should set ourselves on fire in the service of Hashem? Woe for such a question, and woe for the answer!

Seeing that he started out by bringing proofs for his arguments that had no bearing on the subject and ended up by approving the views of heretics and Christians, I thought it appropriate to apply this verse to him, *"His talk begins as silliness and ends as disastrous madness" (Koheles 10:13)*.

No one has the right to speak and deliver sermons in public before he has gone over his speech two, three and four times and then reviewed it thoroughly. The Sages derived this from Scriptural verse, *"Then He saw it and gauged it; He measured it and probed it."* And afterward, *"He said to man" (Iyov 28:27)*. This is what a person needs to do before he speaks. But the things a person writes down with his own hand and inscribes in a book, he should review a thousand times, if possible. This man did nothing of the kind. He recorded all these important ideas in a document, but did not prepare a first draft nor edit it. He considered his statements beyond doubt. They did not need to be checked. He handed them to someone who brought them to every city and province. He brought darkness into the hearts of the people, as it says *"He sent darkness, and it was very dark" (Tehillim 105:28)*.

The Gravity of Maligning a Jew

I will now begin to outline the magnitude of the error that this poor creature committed, and the [damage] he caused through his ignorance. He meant to do good, but instead he caused harm [by making statements] that are not substantiated. His long drawn out prose demonstrates self-love of his own style of writing.

It is well known from the commentaries of our Sages that in *Moshe's* time, before the Exodus, the people of Yisrael had gone astray and broken the covenant of *bris milah*. None except for the tribe of Levi, were circumcised *(Shemos Rabbah 19:6)*. [This situation prevailed] until the mitzvah of *Pesach* was announced. Hashem said to Moshe *"No uncircumcised may eat it" (Shemos 12:43)*. He then told them to perform the *milah* — circumcision. Our Rabbis give an account of the procedure: Moshe did the circumcision, Yehoshua performed the *periah*, and Aharon did the *metzitzah*[1]. Then they piled the foreskins in heaps. The blood of *milah* became mixed with the blood of the

---

1. *periah*-revealing the corona and *metzitzah*-sucking the blood are essential parts of the *milah*.

korban Pesach (the paschal lamb), and this made them worthy to be redeemed. This is the meaning of Hashem's message to *Yechezkel, "When I passed by you and saw you wallowing in your blood, I said to you, 'Live by your blood;' yea, I said to you, 'Live by your blood'"* (Yechezkel 16:6). Our Sages remark that [the Jewish people] had become debased with incest, as it is described [in the chapter[2] that begins with] *"Once there were two women, daughters of one mother"* (Yechezkel 23:2).

Although they were perverted to such an extent, when Moshe said, *"But they will not believe me" (Shemos 4:1),* Hashem admonishes him saying, "Moshe, they are believers, children of believers; believers, for it says, *'and the people believed' (Shemos 14:31);* sons of believers, for it says, *'He [Avraham] believed in Hashem, and He counted it as righteousness' (Bereishis 15:6).* But you [Moshe] will end up not believing, as it says, *'You did not have enough faith in Me to sanctify Me'" (Bamidbar 20:12).* As a matter of fact, [Moshe] was punished immediately, as the Rabbis expounded, "He who suspects the innocent is punished physically. From where is this derived? From Moshe[3]".

In the same vein, in *Eliyahu's* days, they all willfully worshiped idols, except for *"the seven thousand—every knee that has not knelt to Baal and every mouth that has not kissed him" (Melachim I 19:18).* Nevertheless, when [Eliyahu] accused Yisrael at *Chorev,* he was taken to task for it, as can be gathered from the verse, "[Hashem said to him], *'Why are you here Eliyahu?'* He replied, *'I am moved by zeal for Hashem, the God of Hosts,*

---

2. In this chapter, Yechezkel describes in detail the depraved conduct of the kingdoms of Yehudah and Yisrael.

3. The Torah relates that immediately after Moshe made this comment, his hand was struck with leprosy.

for the Israelites have forsaken Your covenant, torn down Your altars, and put Your prophets to the sword. I alone am left, and they are out to take my life" (Melachim I 19:9,10).

[The Sages interpret this verse as a dialogue between Hashem and Eliyahu. Eliyahu: They have forsaken Your covenant.]

Hashem: Is it your covenant by any chance?

Eliyahu: They also tore down Your altars.

Hashem: Were they your altars perhaps?

Eliyahu: They put Your prophets to the sword.

Hashem: But you are still alive!

Eliyahu: I alone am left, and they are out to take my life.

Hashem: Instead of accusing Yisrael, shouldn't you rather denounce the gentile nations? They maintain a house of debauchery, a house of idol worship, and you indict Yisrael! *"Forsake the cities of Aroer"* (Yeshaya 17:2). *"Go back by the way you came, and on to the wilderness of Damascus"* (Melachim I 19:15). This is all explained by the Rabbis in Midrash Chazisa (Shir Hashirim Rabbah 1:6).

Likewise, in *Yeshayah's* days, the Jewish people were deeply steeped in sin, as it says, *"Ah, sinful nation! People laden with iniquity! (Yeshayah 1:4).* They worshiped idols, as it says, *"Behind the door and doorpost you have directed your thoughts" (Yeshayah 57:8).* There were also murderers among them, as it says, *"Alas, she has become a harlot, the faithful city that was filled with justice, where righteousness dwelt—but now murderers" (Yeshayah 1:21).* They also desecrated God's Name, saying, *"Eat and drink for tomorrow we shall die" (Yeshayah 22:13).* They treated Hashem's mitzvos with contempt, saying, *"Leave the way! Get off the path! Let us hear no more about the Holy One of Yisrael" (Yeshayah 30:11).*

In spite of all this, when Yeshaya said *"And I live among a people of unclean lips,"* he was punished immediately, as it says *"one of the seraphs flew over to me with a live coal . . . He touched it to my lips and declared, 'Now that this has touched your lips, your guilt shall depart and your sin purged away'" (Yeshayah 6:5-7).* According to the Sages, his sin was not forgiven until Menashe killed him (Sanhedrin 103b).

When the angel appeared and pleaded unfavorably against Yehoshua the son of Yehotzadak because his sons had married women who were unsuitable to be the wives of priests, Hashem distanced himself from the angel as it is written, *"Hashem rebuke you, O Satan, may Hashem Who has chosen Jerusalem rebuke you! For this is a brand plucked from the fire" (Zechariah 3:2).*

This is the kind of punishment that has been meted out to the pillars of the world—Moshe, Eliyahu, Yeshayah, and the ministering angels—for speaking just a few disparaging words about the Jewish people. You can imagine [what will happen to] the least among the lowly if he unleashes his tongue and speaks out against Jewish communities, rabbis and their students, priests and Levites, calling them sinners, evildoers, disqualified to testify as witnesses, and heretics who deny Hashem the God of Yisrael. Remember, the writer recorded these [slanderous remarks] in his own handwriting! Just think what his punishment will be! [The forced converts] did not rebel against God to seek pleasure and enjoyment. They did not abandon the Jewish religion to attain status and mundane delights. *"For they have fled before swords, before the whetted sword, before the bow that was drawn, before the stress of war' (Yeshayah 21:15).* This man did not realize that these were not willful transgressors. Hashem will not abandon or forsake them, *"for he did not scorn, He did not spurn the plea of the poor" (Tehillim 22:25).* Concerning such people the Torah says, *"[Yitzchak] smelled the fragrance of his (Yaakov's) clothes" (Bereishis 27:27)*. Said the Sages, "Instead of reading *begadav* (his clothes), read *bogdav*[4]" (those that deceive him)" *[Bereishis Rabbah 65]*.

Whatever this man said are things he dreamed up. During one of the persecutions in which the great rabbis were killed, Rabbi Meir was arrested. People who knew him said, "You are Meir, aren't you?" and he replied, "No, I am not." Pointing at the meat of a pig they ordered, "Eat this if you are not a Jew." He answered, "I'll be glad to eat it", and made believe he was eating but in fact did not *(Avodah Zarah 16b-18)*. No doubt, in the view of this "humble" person who knows the true meaning of the Torah[5], Rabbi Meir who worshipped Hashem secretly is considered a gentile, since in his responsum he writes, that whoever acts publicly like a gentile while secretly behaving like a Jew, is a gentile.

There is also the famous story of how Rabbi Eliezer was seized by heretics, whose offense is worse than idolatry. The heretics—may Hashem cut them down—ridicule all religion and say such things as, "Believers are fools!", "Students of religion are crazy!" They deny prophecy entirely. Rabbi Eliezer was a famous scholar in the sciences. They asked him, "How can you have reached such a high level of scholarship and still believe in religion?" He answered them, appearing to have adopted their creed, whereas he really had in mind the true faith and no other.

This story is told in the Midrash *(Koheles Rabbah 1:8)*

---

4. The word *begadav* (his clothes) has the same letters as *bogdav* (his deception); and the verse ends "and he (Yitzchak) blessed him." The underlying idea is that even when the Jewish people (Yaakov) transgress Hashem's laws, they remain His children and will receive His blessing.

5. The Rambam is writing this sarcastically.

as follows: It happened that Rabbi Eliezer was seized [by heretics] in order to convert him to heresy. The general brought him to the capital and said, "How is it that an old man like you spends his time on things like that?" He replied, "I accept the judge's words as the truth." The general thought that he meant him, whereas he was really referring to Hashem. The general then said, "Rabbi, I see you have faith in me . . ." [turning to his men he said,] "I really was wondering, how could he have been led astray by such things?" Thereupon he said [to Rabbi Eliezer,] "I pardon you. You are free to go!"

You see that Rabbi Eliezer pretended to the general that he was a heretic,although in his heart he was devoted to Hashem. Heresy is much more serious than idolatry, as has been outlined throughout the Talmud. Yet according to the writings of this "devout" individual, Rabbi Eliezer should be disqualified. In this current persecution, [our transgression is far less serious,] we do not pretend that we are idol worshippers, we only declare that we believe their creed. They are well aware that we do not believe one word of it. We are saying so only to deceive the king, similar to what the prophet said, "Yet they deceived him with their speech, lied to him with their words" (Tehillim 78:36).

It is well known what happened to the Jewish people in the days of the evil Nebuchadnezzar. The entire population of Babylon, except *Chanaiah, Mishael* and *Azariah,* bowed to the statue. Hashem testified about that generation, stating, "No more shall Yaakov be shamed, no longer his face grow pale" (Yeshayah 29:22). Even the great Torah scholars, if they were present at the time, perhaps bowed down [to the image] in Babylon. I have not come across anyone who called them wicked, gentiles or disqualified to testify as witnesses. Neither has Hashem counted their action as the sin of idolatry, because they were forced to do it. The Sages confirm this, with reference to the time of Haman, saying, "They performed [the act of prostrating themselves] outwardly, I will also deal with them only outwardly" (*Megillah 12a*).

The author of this response is no doubt a God-fearing man; [he should take a lesson from the Almighty how to treat his people.] *"Shame on him who argues with his Maker, a potsherd with the potsherds of earth! Shall the clay say to the potter, 'What are you doing?'"* (*Yeshayah 45:9*).

It is known what happened to the Jewish people under the wicked rule of the Greeks. Harsh and evil decrees were issued. There even was a rule that no one was allowed to close the door of his house, so that he would not be alone and be able to fulfill a mitzvah. In spite of this the Sages did not consider them gentiles or evildoers, but completely righteous. They pleaded for them to Hashem and added in the special prayer of thanksgiving, *Al Hanissim*—"For the Miracles"—the phrase, "and the wicked in the hands of the **righteous[6].**"

6. Namely that the Greeks who were wicked were delivered into the hands of the Jews who were righteous, although they had transgressed the mitzvos out of duress.

The Importance of Every Mitzvah

Purpose of this Letter

If not for the fact that in my introductory remarks I resolved not to quote all the things this man has written, I would show you in detail how this person made a fool of himself. He, not only said things that are foolish, but even took a pen in hand and wrote them down. In response to a question, he cited material that is totally beside the point. He brings proof from the laws of *eidim zomemim*—"the refuted witnesses" (See *Devarim 19:15-21*), from one who curses his father or mother, the mitzvah of *tzitzis*, the prohibition of plowing with an ox and a donkey together, and the prohibition of crossbreeding one's livestock with other species, as if the questioner had asked him to compile *Azharos*[1] for him and list all the mitzvos.

Then he says that the Moslems have an idol in

---

1.   Azharos is a list of the 613 mitzvos.

Mecca and in other places. Did the questioner ask whether or not he should go on a pilgrimage to Mecca? He also states that the Madman (Mohammed) killed 24,000 Jews, as if he was asked whether Mohammed has a share in the world-to-come.

There are many more such irrelevant statements. This man really should have heeded Shlomoh's counsel, *"Keep your mouth from being rash, and let not your throat be quick to bring forth speech before God" (Koheles 5:1).* Had he paid attention to this verse, he would have realized that whoever answered or analyzed a question regarding permitted and forbidden things was interpreting God's word. He would not have blundered the way he did.

[Although I take issue with his accusation against the Jewish people], Hashem knows and is a good witness, that even if he had insulted people more than he did and had babbled more than he did, it would not hurt me. I am not looking for any support. On the contrary, I think, *"Let us lie down in our shame, let our disgrace cover us; for we have sinned against the Lord our God, we and our fathers (Yirmiyah 3:25).* I would have held him in great esteem and I would have said that he acted for the sake of Heaven. For, thank God, I know my worth, and I would not have made a fool of him. *"We acknowledge our wickedness, O Hashem—the iniquity of our fathers" (Yirmiyah 14:20).* But it would not have been right for me to look away and to keep quiet, since he said that any forced convert who prays receives no reward for his prayer but has, on the contrary, committed a sin [by praying]. I know that whatever is published in a book—whether it is true or false—will surely influence a wide readership. This is why so many wrong ideas circulate among people. The only way that a false idea reaches you is by way of a written book. Therefore, I was afraid that this response that turns people away from Hashem will fall into the hands of an unlearned person. He will read that he will receive no reward for praying, and he will not pray. He will reason that, in the same way, he will not be rewarded for performing any of the mitzvos. Eventually, this idea will surely lead to the creation of a new sect.

Refutation of the Rabbi's Response

I will now explain where this bombastic babbler slipped up. We read in *Tanach* a detailed account how *Achav*, the son of Omri, denied God and worshiped idols, as Hashem testifies, *"Indeed there never was anyone like Achav who sold himself to do evil in the eyes of Hashem" (Melachim I 21:25)*. He fasted two and a half hours and had the decree against him annulled (Taanis 25b), as it says, *"Then the word of Hashem came to Eliyahu the Tishbite, 'Have you seen how Achav has humbled himself before Me? Because he has humbled himself before Me, I will not bring disaster in his lifetime; I will bring disaster upon his house in his son's time'" (Melachim I 21:28-29)*.

Eglon, the king of Moab, oppressed Yisrael, yet he was richly rewarded by God because he paid homage to Him. He rose from his seat when Ehud said to him, *"I have a message for you from God" (Shoftim 3:20)*. Hashem rewarded him and preordained that the throne of Shlomoh which is Hashem's throne, as it says, *"And Shlomoh sat on Hashem's throne" (Divrei Hayamim I 29:23)*, and the throne of King Mashiach would come from [Eglon's] descendants. [Our sages teach us that] Ruth the Moabite, great grandmother of King David, was Eglon's daughter (*Sanhedrin 105b*).

The Rabbis noted that Hashem did not withhold his reward.

The wicked Nebuchadnezzar who killed countless Jews and burned the House that is the footstool of God was rewarded with forty years of royal rule like Shlomoh, because he ran four paces in order to place the name of God before the name of *Chizkiyahu* (Sanhedrin 96a). Again, Hashem did not withhold his reward.

The wicked *Eisav* was detested by Hashem, as He testifies, *"And I have hated Eisav" (Malachi 1:3)*. The Sages outline his crimes as follows, "That day, he committed five sins: he murdered, worshiped idols, raped an engaged girl, denied resurrection, and rejected his birthright. He then [deceived his father] by wrapping himself in his *tallis*, entering his father Yitzchak's room and saying to him, 'Father, does the law of tithing apply to salt?' Said Yitzchak [to himself], 'How carefully my son observes the mitzvos!'". Even so, as the reward for the one mitzvah—that of honoring his father—which he fulfilled, Hashem granted him uninterrupted kingship until the coming of King Mashiach. Our Sages say, "David's descendant (Mashiach) will not come before Eisav receives his reward for the mitzvah of honoring ones father and mother. They derived this from the verse, *"After honor he sent me unto the nations[2]" (Zechariah 2:12)*. Our Sages formulated this idea in the following terms, "The Holy One, Blessed is He, does not deprive any creature of the reward due to it" (Pesachim 118a). He always rewards everyone for the good deeds he performs and punishes everyone for his misdeed; as long as he continues to do it.

---

2. Our Sages interpreted this verse as follows—after the reward given to Eisav for honoring his father will Yisrael be sent unto the nations.

Now if these well-known heretics were richly rewarded by Hashem for the little good they did, how can Hashem not reward Jews who were forced to convert but who nevertheless perform the mitzvos secretly. Can it be that Hashem does not distinguish between one who performs a mitzvah and one who does not, or between one who serves Hashem and one who does not? This man says [the opposite], that when he prays he commits a sin, and he backs this up by quoting the verse, *"For my people has done a twofold wrong"* (Yirmiyah 2:13). Now we have explained his error. He defames his contemporaries, and speaks contrary to the words of the rabbis, as we mentioned. He is even maligning the Creator, stating that He punishes a person for performing mitzvos. He stated, in fact, that the prayer of any of you is considered a sin. Shlomoh had such a situation in mind when he said, *"And don't plead before the messenger that it was an error"* (Koheles 5:5).

When I realized that this matter was a disease for the eyes, I set myself to gather herbs and choice spices from the books of the ancient pharmacists with which to concoct a medicine and an eye ointment for this disease. With God's help, it will bring about a cure.[3]

---

3. The Rambam who was a famous physician uses a pharmaceutical metaphor to introduce his exhaustive response to the question regarding forced conversion to Islam.

Discussion of Kiddush Hashem

It is useful to divide my remarks on this subject into five parts: 1. The obligation to mitzvos during times of compulsion. 2. Parameters of *Chillul Hashem*—desecration of Hashem's Name—and its punishment. 3. The status of one who gives his life *al Kiddush Hashem*—for the sanctification of Hashem's name—and of one who transgresses under duress. 4. How the present persecution differs from previous ones, and how one should act during this situation. 5. How a person should perceive himself during this persecution, may Hashem end it soon. Amen.

I: The Obligation to Mitzvos during times of Religious Compulsion

The three prohibitions of idolatry, incest, and manslaughter, have a particular stringency. Whenever a person is forced to violate any of these, he is at all times, everywhere, and under all circumstances, commanded to give up his life rather than transgress. When I say, "at all times" I mean in a time of persecution or otherwise; when I say "everywhere" I mean in private or in public; when I say, "under all circumstances" I mean whether the oppressor intends to make him violate his religious beliefs or not. [In any of these situations], he must choose death.

If he is forced to transgress any other commandment, excluding the aforementioned three, he must evaluate the circumstances. If the oppressor does it for his own benefit, be it at a time of persecution or not, privately or publicly, he may violate the law and thereby save his life. This may be found in the Talmud (Sanhedrin 74b) "But Esther was [forced to sin] in public ? Abaye said, 'Esther was passive.' Rava said, 'If it is for his own enjoyment it makes a difference.'" We have a standing rule that the Halachah is decided according to Rava.

To summarize, if the oppressor is doing it for his personal benefit one should transgress and avoid being killed, even if it is in public and during a time of persecution.

If the oppressor intends to make him [violate his beliefs] and commit a sin, he must evaluate [the times]. In a time of persecution he must give up his life and not transgress, whether in private or in public. If it is not a time of persecution, he should transgress and save his life, if it is in private, but he should choose death if it is in public.

This is the relevant text in the Talmud; "When Rav Dimi (Ravin) arrived, he said in the name of Rabbi Yochanan that even if it is not a time of persecution, he may transgress and not die, only in private; in public he may not violate even a minor mitzvah, even changing the way he ties his shoes". By "in public" is meant [in the presence of] ten Jewish males.

II: Parameters of Chillul Hashem and its Punishment

The parameters of *Chillul Hashem*—desecration of Hashem's Name can be divided into two categories: one that applies to [the] general [populace] and one to specific [people].

That which applies to the general populace takes two forms. The first form: When a person commits a sin out of spite, not for the pleasure or enjoyment to be derived from that act, but because he treats it lightly and disdainfully, he is thereby desecrating Hashem's Name. Hashem says concerning one who swears falsely, which is an act that brings him no pleasure or enjoyment, *"Do not swear falsely by My Name; [if you do so] you will be desecrating your God's Name"* (Vayikra 19:12). If he does it in public he is openly desecrating Hashem's Name. I explained above that "in public" means in the presence of ten Jews.

The second form: When someone consciously fails to correct his behavior to the point that people begin to talk disparagingly about him. He may not have committed a sin, but he has nonetheless desecrated Hashem's Name. When he is [being percieved as] sinning by his fellow man, a person should be as careful as he is of sinning to his Creator, for Hashem said, *"You shall be innocent before Hashem and Yisrael"* (Bamidbar 32:22).

The Talmud (Yoma 86a) asks regarding this subject, ["What is meant by chillul Hashem?"] Rav Nachman bar Yitzchak replied, "For example, if people say about someone, May God forgive so-and-so". Another example cited is, "When friends are embarrassed by his reputation."

The parameters of chillul Hashem which apply to

specific people also takes two forms:

The first form: When a learned person does something that a person of his stature should not do, even though others may do so without compunction. Because he has a reputation of being a man of virtue, people expect more of him. [By his action] he has desecrated Hashem's Name. Rav gave the following definition of chillul Hashem, "For example, when I buy meat and do not pay right away" (Yoma 86a). In other words, a person of his eminence should not buy anything unless he pays immediately, at the time of purchase, although the practice [of buying on credit] is quite acceptable with the general public. Rabbi Yochanan said the following on the subject, "For example, if I walk four ells without wearing my tefillin and without being engrossed in Torah thoughts [it is considered a chillul Hashem]". He is referring to a man of his stature. Very often we find that the Talmud draws a distinction when the person is an important personality.

The second form: When a learned man behaves in a lowly and loathsome way in his dealings with people. He receives people angrily and with contempt. He is not genial with people and does not treat them with decency and respect. Such a person has desecrated Hashem's Name. The Sages phrased it this way, "When a person is learned but is not honest in his dealings with people and does not speak gently to people, what do people say about him? Woe is to so-and-so who studied Torah!"

If I were not concerned about being long-winded and going off on a tangent, I would explain to you how a person should behave toward others, what his actions and words should be like and how he should receive people. Thus anyone who spoke to him or had dealings with him would speak about him only in glowing terms. I would explain the meaning of the phrases "being honest in one's dealings with people" and "speaking gently to people." But this would require a full-length book. So I will pick up where I left off.

Kiddush Hashem—Sanctification of Hashem's Name is the opposite of Chillul Hashem. When a person fulfills a mitzvah and is inspired by no other motive than his love of Hashem and the desire to serve Him, he has publicly sanctified Hashem's Name. So too, if good things are said about him, he has sanctified Hashem's Name. The Sages phrased it like this, "When a person has studied Torah and Mishnah, attended to Torah scholars and dealt gently with people, what do people say about him? 'See how pleasant is his conduct, how seemly are his deeds!'" Scripture says this about such a man, *"And He said to me, 'You are My servant, Yisrael in whom I glory'" (Yeshayah 49:3)*. Regarding Kiddush Hashem a great person is also special. If a great man avoids distasteful situations he is sanctifying Hashem's Name. And so we read, *"Put crooked speech away from you" (Mishlei 4:24)*.

Chillul Hashem is a grave sin. Both the deliberate sinner and the inadvertent sinner are punished. The Rabbis phrased it succinctly, "Both unintentional and intentional, are liable regarding desecration of the Name" *(Avos 4:5)*. A man is granted a delay in punishment for all sins, but not for the desecration of Hashem's Name. The Rabbis stated, "For the desecration of Hashem's Name no credit is extended. What do we mean that no credit is extended? He is not treated as he is by the storekeeper who extends credit" *(Kiddushin 40a)*. In other words, he will be required to pay for his transgression immediately. The Sages also teach that, "Whoever desecrates Hashem's Name in secret, is punished in public" *(Avos 4:5)*.

This sin is more serious than any other. Neither Yom Kippur, nor suffering, nor repentance can atone for chillul Hashem. This is what the Rabbis say about it, "He who is guilty of chillul Hashem cannot have his sin erased by either repentance, Yom Kippur or through suffering; they all suspend punishment until death affords forgiveness, for so it says, *"Then the Lord of Hosts revealed Himself to my ears: 'This iniquity shall never be forgiven you until you die'"* (Yeshayah 22:14). This entire discourse refers to the person who willingly desecrates the Name of Hashem, as I shall explain.

Just as chillul Hashem is a grave sin, so is *kiddush Hashem*—the Sanctification of Hashem's Name—a great mitzvah for which you are richly rewarded. Every Jew is required to sanctify Hashem's Name. It is written in Sifra, *"I am Hashem your God, who brought you out of the land of Egypt to give you the land of Canaan, [and] to be a God for you"* (Vayikra 25:38), on condition that you sanctify My Name publicly. We also find in the Talmud *(Sanhedrin 74b)* it says, "Rabbi Ami was asked, Is a Noachide commanded to sanctify Hashem's Name?" With regard to a Jew this question was not raised, obviously it may be inferred that a Jew is indeed commanded to sanctify His Name, as it is stated, *"I must be sanctified among the Israelites"* (Vayikra 22:32).

III: The Status of one who gives his life al Kiddush Hashem and of one who Transgresses under Duress

You must realize that wherever the Sages ruled that one must give up his life rather than transgress, and he does so, he has sanctified Hashem's name. If ten Jews witnessed his death he has sanctified the Name publicly. For example: *Chananiah, Mishael* and *Azariah,*[1] Daniel,[2] the Ten Martyrs killed by the Romans[3], the seven sons of *Channah*[4] and all the other Jews who gave their lives for the sanctification of the Name, may the Merciful one speedily avenge their blood. The following verse applies to them, *"Bring in My devotees, who made a covenant with Me over sacrifice"* (Tehillim 50:5). Our Rabbis related the following verse to them, *"I adjure you, O maidens of Jerusalem, by gazelles or by hinds of the fields"* (Shir Hashirim 2:7). They expounded, *"I adjure you O maidens of Jerusalem"*—the persecuted generations; *"by the gazelles"*—those who did for Me what I desired, and I did what they desired; *"by the hinds of the field"*—those who shed their blood for Me like the blood of gazelles and hinds. The following verse also applies to them: *"It is for Your sake*

---

1. See Daniel, chapter 3. Nebuchadnezzar ordered everyone to bow down before a huge statue, but Daniel's three friends refused to do so. They were thrown into a furnace but were miraculously saved.
2. Daniel who disobeyed King Darius' order and prayed to Hashem was miraculously saved from the lion's den into which he was thrown.
3. The story of the ten great Tanna'im who were brutally killed by the Romans is told in the *Eileh Ezkera*, recited on Yom Kippur during Mussaf.
4. They were killed by Antiochus, in the times of Chanukah, for refusing to worship the Greek idol.

that we are slain all day long" (Tehillim 44:23).

A person to whom God granted the privilege to rise to the lofty level of dying *al kiddush Hashem* — for the Sanctification of Hashem's Name, although he may not have been a Torah scholar, merits to be in the world to come, even if he was sinful as *Yerovam ben Nevat* and his colleagues. The Rabbis say of this, "'No one can approach the high rank of those martyred by the government!' Who are we referring to? We cannot say that this refers to Rabbi Akiva and his colleagues [who were martyrs of the Roman government], because surely they had other claims to eminence. It must be referring to the martyrs of Lydda[5]."

If one did not allow himself to be killed, but under duress transgressed and remained alive, he did not do the right thing. Under duress he desecrated Hashem's Name. However, he does not incur any of the seven penalties enumerated in the Torah, namely: the four death penalties of the human court [stoning, burning, beheading and strangling]; premature death; *Kareis*—divinely caused death; and lashes. There is not a single case in the entire Torah in which a person acting under duress is sentenced to any of these punishments, whether his transgression was minor or major. Only a willful sinner is punished, not one who was forced. As it says, *"However, if a person commits [an act of idolatry] highhandedly, whether he is a native born or a proselyte, he is blaspheming Hashem, and that person shall be cut off [spiritually] from among his people" (Bamidbar 15:30).* The Talmud is full of statements to the effect that a person acting under duress is not guilty.

---

5. Two brothers, Lulianus and Pappus, who took upon themselves the guilt for the death of the Emperor's daughter, in order to save the entire nation. See Taanis 18b.

According to the Torah, ". . . *this case[6] is no different from the case where a man rises up against his neighbor and murders him" (Devarim 22:26).* We often read in the Talmud, "According to the Torah, a person who acted under duress, is exempt from punishment." He is not characterized as a sinner or a wicked man, and he is not disqualified [by this] from serving as a witness. Only if he [willfully] committed a sin that disqualifies him from serving as a witness. [All that can be said is that] he did not fulfill the mitzvah of *kiddush Hashem*, but under no circumstances can he be considered as having willfully desecrated Hashem's Name.

Whoever says or thinks that a person should be sentenced to death because he violated a law of which the Sages said that he should give up his life rather than transgress, is completely wrong. It simply is not so, as I will explain. What is meant is that it is a mitzvah to offer his life, but if he did not, he is not liable to the death penalty. And even if he was forced to worship idols he is not liable to *kareis* (be cut off spiritually). He certainly is not executed by order of the court. This principle is clearly stated in *Toras Kohanim*: "Hashem says [concerning a man who gives any of his children to Molech[7],] *"I will direct My anger against that person" (Vayikra 20:5).* Our sages comment, "but not if he was forced, acted unwittingly, or was misled." It is clear then that if he was forced or misled he is not liable. We are speaking about a prohibition, that had it been done intentionally has the stringency of Kareis. Certainly, if he was forced to commit sins that when

---

6.   The Torah is relating the punishment for one who forcibly cohabits with a betrothed girl. The Torah specifically excludes the girl from punishment, although technically she was involved in adultery.

7.   A form of idol worship.

done intentionally are punishable by lashes, he is not at all liable. The prohibition of *chillul Hashem* is a negative commandment, [that is not liable Kareis]. As it is stated, *"Do not desecrate My holy Name" (Vayikra 22:32)*. [Surely one who transgresses under duress is not liable.]

It is a known fact that making a false oath is a desecration of Hashem's Name. As it says, *"Do not swear falsely by My Name; [if you do], you will be desecrating your God's Name. I am Hashem" (Vayikra 19:12)*. Still, the Mishnah reads, "One is allowed to vow to murderers, robbers and tax-collectors that what he has is *terumah*[8], [thereby saving his produce]. Beis Shammai states that one may only use the form of a *neder* (vow). Beis Hillel says that one may also use the formula of *shevuah* (oath)" (Nedarim 3:4).

These things are clearly spelled out. There is no need to bring any proofs to support them; how can anyone say that the law regarding a person who acted under duress and one who acted voluntarily is the same? Our Sages ruled in many cases, "Let him transgress and not give up his life." Now this man [who wrote this response] considers himself to be more worthy than the Rabbis and more scrupulous in the observance of the mitzvos. He openly declares his willingness to surrender his life in all cases and thinks that he is sanctifying Hashem's Name. However, if he would indeed act this way [and surrender his life in every instance] he would be a sinful and rebellious individual. He would bear guilt for his soul, for Hashem said, *"Keep My decrees and laws, since by keeping them a person will live" (Vayikra 18:5)*—and not die (Sanhedrin 74a).

---

8. Produce permitted only to a Kohain.

IV: How this Persecution Differs from Previous Ones and How One Should Act During the Present Situation

You have to realize that in all the persecutions that occurred in the time of the Sages, they were ordered to violate mitzvos and to perform [sinful] acts, as we are told in the Talmud: They were forbidden to study Torah and to circumcise their sons. They were ordered to have intercourse with their wives when they were ritually unclean. But in the present persecution they are not required to do any forbidden action, only to say something. If a person wishes to fulfill the 613 commandments of the Torah in secret he can do so. He is not guilty of anything unless he happens to desecrate the Shabbos without being forced to do so. This oppressive regime does not force anyone to do any prohibited act, just to make an oral affirmation [of faith]. They know very well that we do not mean what we say, and that the person making the affirmation is only doing so to escape the king's wrath and to satisfy him with a recitation of meaningless incantations.

If anyone asks me whether he should offer his life or make this acknowledgement, I tell him to acknowledge and not choose death. However if one died a martyr's death rather than affirm the divine mission of "that man" (Mohammed), we can say that he acted righteously. He will receive an abundant reward from Hashem. His position will be in the loftiest levels, for he has given his life for the sanctity of Hashem. However, one should not stay in the country under the rule of that king. [Until he is able to leave], he should stay home, do his work secretly and go out only if it is absolutely essential.

There has never been a persecution as unusual as this, where people are only compelled to say something. Our Rabbis ruled that a person should choose death and not transgress. We cannot infer that they meant speech that does not involve action. One must submit to martyrdom only when he is forced to do something that he is forbidden to do.

A person who is caught in this persecution should conduct himself along the following lines: Let him set his sights on observing as many of the mitzvos as he can. If he transgressed often or desecrated the Shabbos, he should still not carry what he is not allowed to carry[9]. He should not say to himself, "The transgressions I have made are more grave than [the carrying on Shabbos] from which I am abstaining now." Let him be as careful about observing the mitzvos as he can.

A person must be aware of this fundamental Torah principle. Yerovam ben Nevat and others like him are punished for [the grievous sin of] making the calves as well as for disregarding the [comparatively minor] law of *eiruv tavshilin*[10] and similar laws. Don't say that to him applies the rule of "he who has committed two offenses must be held answerable for the more severe one only"*(Gittin 52b)*. This principle applies only to punishments meted out by man in this world. Hashem metes out punishment for minor and serious sins, and He rewards people for everything they do. A person

---

9. On Shabbos it is forbidden to carry an object from a private domain into a public domain, or vice versa, or to carry an object four ells in a public domain.
10. Eiruv tavshilin, the law of "combination of dishes." When a *Yom Tov* falls on Friday, it is forbidden to cook or bake for Shabbos unless an eiruv tavshilin is performed.

should be aware that he is held accountable for every transgression he committed. He is rewarded for every mitzvah he performed. Things are not the way people think.

The recommendation I followed myself, and the advice I want to give to all my friends and anyone that consults me, is to leave those places and to go to where we can practice our religion and fulfill the Torah without compulsion and fear. Let him leave his family and his possessions. The Law of Hashem that He has given us as a heritage is very great. Our commitment to it takes precedence to material values. All thinkers scorn material wealth, which is transitory, but the fear of Hashem endures.

Let us say, there were two Jewish cities, one superior to the other in its deeds and conduct, more meticulous with mitzvos and more dedicated to their observance. A God-fearing person is required to leave the city where the actions are not quite proper and move to the better city. Our Sages admonished us in this regard, stating, "You should not live in a city where there are fewer than ten righteous residents." They find support for this in the verse, [where Abraham pleads with Hashem to spare the city of Sodom, saying,] *"Suppose there are ten [righteous people] found there?"* And He answered, *"I will not destroy for the sake of the ten" (Bereishis 18:32).* This is what one should do when both cities are Jewish. Certainly, if a Jew lives in a place inhabited by gentiles, he must leave it and go to a more favorable place. He must make every effort to do so, although he may place himself in jeopardy. He must escape that bad place where he cannot practice his religion properly, and set out until he arrives at a decent place.

The prophets have postulated that he who lives

among heretics is considered one of them. They derived it from [The words of King David who said, when he was banished from Eretz Yisrael], *"For they have driven me out today, so that I cannot have a share in Hashem's possession, rather I am told, 'Go and worship other gods' "(Shmuel I 26:19).* You see that [David] equates his dwelling among gentiles with the worship of other gods. In the same vein, David says, *"O Lord, You know I hate those who hate You and loathe Your adversaries" (Tehillim 139:21),* and also, *"I am a companion to all who fear You, to those who keep Your precepts" (Tehillim 119:63).* Similarly, we see that our father Abraham despised his family and his home town. He ran for his life to escape from the creed of the heretics.

He should make an effort to leave the non-believer's environment when they do not force him to follow in their ways. But when they coerce him to transgress even one of the mitzvos he is forbidden to remain in that place. He must leave and abandon everything he owns, travel day and night, until he finds a spot where he can practice his religion. There is a big, wide world out there!

The excuse of the person who claims that he has to take care of his family and his household really does not hold water. *"A brother cannot redeem a man or pay his ransom to God" (Tehillim 49:8).* In my opinion, it is not right to make this claim to avoid the obligation. He should emigrate to a decent place, and under no circumstances continue to stay in the land of persecution. Whoever remains there is a transgressor and desecrates Hashem's Name, and is almost an intentional sinner.

There are those who delude themselves into believing that they should remain where they are until King Mashiach comes to the lands of the Maghreb. Then they will go to Jerusalem. I do not know how they will disentangle themselves from the present persecution. They are transgressors, and they cause others to sin. The prophet Yirmiyah had people like them in mind when he said, *"They offer healing offhand for the wounds of My people, saying, 'all is well, all is well"* *(Yirmiyah 6:14).* There is no dependable set time for the coming of Mashiach. One does not know if he is coming soon or in the distant future. The obligation of keeping the mitzvos is not dependent on the coming of Mashiach. We are required to engross ourselves in Torah and mitzvos. We must strive to achieve perfection in both of them. Then, if Hashem grants us, our children or grandchildren the privilege to witness the coming of Mashiach, so much the better. If he does not come we have not lost anything. On the contrary, we have gained by doing what we had to do.

A person may be in a place where he sees Torah study coming to an end, the Jewish population declining and gradually disappearing, and he himself unable to practice his religion. He says, "I am going to stay here until Mashiach comes. Then I will be extricated from this predicament." Such a person is guilty of wickedness, destructive callousness and of wiping out the Jewish faith and ideology. That is my opinion, and Hashem knows the truth.

V: How a Person Should Perceive Himself During this Persecution

A person may be unable to fulfill the aforementioned advice [to leave the land of persecution], either because of his fondness for his [native] country or because of his fear of the dangers of a sea voyage. He stays where he is. He, then, must regard himself as desecrating Hashem's Name, not quite deliberately, but almost so. He must consider himself as being scolded by God and punished for his bad deeds. At the same time, he should realize that if he performs a mitzvah, the Holy One, Blessed is He, will give him a two-fold reward. He did the mitzvah for the sake of Heaven, and not to impress others or to be regarded as an observant Jew. In addition, a person's reward for performing a mitzvah knowing that if caught, he will lose his life and all his possessions, is much greater than that of a person who fulfills a mitzvah without fear. The Torah, referring to a time like the present, [when observance of mitzvos is done for the sake of heaven and despite the fact that one's life is in danger], says: *"If only you seek Him with all your heart and soul" (Devarim 4:29)*. Nevertheless, you should not take your mind off your plans to leave the provinces that Hashem is angry with, and do your utmost [to carry them out].

It is not right to shun and despise people who desecrate the Shabbos. Rather, you should reach out to them and encourage them to fulfill the mitzvos. The Rabbis ruled that a sinner who willfully transgressed should be welcomed to the synagogue and not humiliated. They based their pronouncement on Shlomoh's advice: *"A thief should not be despised for stealing to appease his hunger" (Mishlei 6:30)*. This means, do not despise sinners in Yisrael when they come secretly to "steal" mitzvos.

Ever since we were banished from our land, persecutions have been our fate, as it says, *"From our youth it (the persecution) raised us as a father and from our mother's womb it has directed us" (Iyov 31:18)*. It also says in many places in the Talmud, "a persecution is likely to pass"(Kesuvos 3b). May Hashem put an end to this one.

"In those days and at that time—declares Hashem—the iniquity of Yisrael shall be sought, and there shall be none; the sins of Yehudah, and none shall be found; for I will pardon those I allow to survive (Yirmiyah 50:12). Let the prophecy be fulfilled speedily in our days. May it be His will. Amen.

Glossary

AL HANISSIM – The Prayer of thanksgiving recited on Chanukah

B'NEI YISRAEL – Children of Israel
BAMIDBAR – The Book of Numbers
BEIS HAMIKDASH – Holy Temple
BEN – son of
BEREISHIS – The Book of Genesis
BILAM – Ballam
BRIS BEIN HABESARIM – Covenant between the halves, a covenant Hashem made with Avraham
BRIS MILAH – Covenant of circumcision

CHILLUL HASHEM – desecration of the name of Hashem

DEVARIM – The Book of Deuteronomy
DIVREI HAYAMIM – The Book of Chronicles

EISAV – Esau
ELIYAHU – Elijah
ERETZ YISRAEL – The Land of Israel

HALACHAH – law
HASHEM – God

IYOV – Job

KAREIS – punishment of premature death
KIDDUSH HASHEM – Sanctification of the name of Hashem
KOHEIN – Priest, descendant of Aaron
KOHELES – Ecclesiastes

LEVI'IM – from the tribe of Levi

MAMZER – illegitimate child
MASHIACH – The Messiah
MELACHIM The Book of Kings

MILAH – circumcision
MISHLEI – Proverbs
MITZVAH pl. *MITZVOS*: – commandment
MOSHE RABBEINU – Moses our Teacher

SHABBOS – The day of rest — Saturday
SHEMOS – The Book of Exodus
SHIR HASHIRIM – Song of Songs
SHLOMOH – Solomon
SHMUEL – The Book of Samuel
SHOFTIM – The Book of Judges
SUKKAH – hut used on Sukkos
SUKKOS – Festival of Tabernacles

TEFILLIN – phylacteries
TEHILLIM – Psalms
TORAS KOHANIM – a commentary from the Sages on the Book of Vayikra
TZITZIS – fringes worn on a four cornered garment

VAYIKRA – The Book of Leviticus

YAAKOV – Jacob
YECHEZKEL – Ezekiel
YEHOSHUA – Joshua
YEROVAM BEN NEVAT – King of the Ten Tribes who broke off from the Kingdom of Judah after the death of Shlomo. In order to stop the people from going to Jerusalem he erected golden calves for them to worship
YESHAYAH – Isaiah
YIRMIYAH – Jeremiah
YERUSHALAYIM – Jerusalem
YISRAEL – Israel
YOEL – Joel